ENGAGING FEMINISM

Students Speak Up & Speak Out

FEMINIST ISSUES: PRACTICE, POLITICS, THEORY
Kathleen M. Balutansky and Alison Booth, editors

Carol Siegel, *Lawrence among the Women:
Wavering Boundaries in Women's Literary Traditions*

Harriet Blodgett, *Capacious Hold-All:
An Anthology of English Women's Diary Writings*

Joy Wiltenburg, *Disorderly Women and Female Power
in the Street Literature of
Early Modern England and Germany*

Diane P. Freedman, *An Alchemy of Genres:
Cross-Genre Writing by American Feminist Poet-Critics*

Jean O'Barr and Mary Wyer, eds., *Engaging Feminism:
Students Speak Up and Speak Out*

ENGAGING FEMINISM

Students Speak Up & Speak Out

EDITED BY JEAN O'BARR & MARY WYER

UNIVERSITY PRESS OF VIRGINIA   CHARLOTTESVILLE AND LONDON

THE UNIVERSITY PRESS OF VIRGINIA
Copyright © 1992 by the Rector and Visitors
of the University of Virginia

First published 1992

Library of Congress Cataloging-in-Publication Data
Engaging feminism : students speak up and speak out / edited by Jean
O'Barr and Mary Wyer.
    p.   cm. — (Feminist issues)
    ISBN 0-8139-1386-1 (cloth). — ISBN 0-8139-1387-X (paper)
    1. Feminism—United States. 2. Women's studies—United States.
3. Women—United States—Social conditions. I. O'Barr, Jean F.
II. Wyer, Mary. III. Series: Feminist issues (Charlottesville, Va.)
HQ1151.E53   1992
305.42′0973—dc20   91-34221
                                                                        CIP

Printed in the United States of America

CONTENTS

CONTENTS

ACKNOWLEDGMENTS

Support for this project came in many forms from many sources, institutional and individual. The friends and alumnae of Duke University who are members of the Friends of Women's Studies, coordinated by the National Council on Women's Studies at Duke University, provided the discretionary monies that were used to bring this project to completion. As a community of professional women, they have endorsed the intellectual and pedagogical directions of the Women's Studies Program with personal commitment and enthusiasm.

The administration at Duke University has been equally supportive, particularly Malcolm Gillis, first as Dean of the Graduate School and now as Dean of the Faculty of Arts and Sciences. His financial support, as well as his determination to see that feminist scholarship has a central place in the university, translates into funds to teach courses, stipends to support graduate students, and a campus climate that enables students to develop their interests in the new research on women.

Four colleagues—Michèl Farrell, Alice Kaplan, Wendy Luttrell, and Sarah Westphal-Wihl—read parts of the manuscript at critical moments, making useful suggestions for revision and urging us onward. Mary Bowman and Connie Pearcy were research assistants who brought their talents and commitments to every task. Nancy Rosebaugh and Vivian Robinson, members of the Women's Studies staff, created a productive work environment in which to sort out the details. We thank you all.

ACKNOWLEDGMENTS

Finally, so that the obvious will not go unsaid, we thank the students, past and present, who breathe life into the Women's Studies Program at Duke University. Sixty students offer writings in this collection, but countless others have engaged us in engaging feminism.

ENGAGING FEMINISM

Students Speak Up & Speak Out

INTRODUCTION

We began this book because we liked the students' writings. Their quality suggested that something useful and productive was going on in our class-rooms, and we wanted others to read and appreciate the students' work as we did. It seemed simple. In retrospect, we had not taken the writings seriously enough. Now after months of discussions about how best to present them to others, we are considering the possibility that we may have opened something of a Pandora's box. We are presenting the ideas, insights, and (yes) critiques of students as if they are of central importance to the educational enterprise, as if we could learn from them. It is all well and good to suggest that students might learn from each other—that a book like *Engaging Feminism* could be a self-help guide for students to learn about women's studies. It is even acceptable to say that women's studies has something to teach all faculty, that we should learn with students, cooperating with them in a common classroom activity.[1] It is another issue altogether to suggest that those teaching in American higher education today, including those in women's studies, would be enriched by a shift in our perspectives on students, to suggest that we might be more effective teachers if our approach was grounded in an appreciation for the knowledge, diversity, and intellectual strengths of those who take our classes. If we listen to what these students/contributors say, they thrive on recognition, appreciation, and trust; they notice their marginalization; and they despair of the waste of their talents.

1

There is evidence in these writings of crossing a milestone on the long road that connects process and content in women's studies. The attempt to make this connection is not a new one. When material on women was first introduced into the classroom, the concern with how to present the material was as central as concerns about what the material should be. Some of the first publications on women's studies as an interdisciplinary subject, in volumes of *Female Studies*, focused on students—on how to engage student energies; how to channel those energies into the personal, political, and scholarly; and how to convince educational institutions that creating and presenting information about women was a valid academic enterprise. Students appeared in these early documents as sources of experiences and as agents for creating more information by reflecting on their experiences and researching women-centered topics. Course syllabi included time for exploring the students' perspectives. Indeed, volume ten of *Female Studies* is an anthology of student writings; some are autobiographical accounts, some are creative works, and some explore relationships with mothers.[2]

Women's studies took a turn in the mid-seventies, however, as the growth of the new scholarship on women became an important and necessary focus of attention. Pedagogical concerns, instead of fueling the debate about women's studies in the academy, became one of many aspects of feminist inquiry. In the next fifteen years, scholars began to recover women's history, women's literature, and both qualitative and quantitative data about women's lives in disciplines as diverse as classics and psychology, religion and medicine, philosophy and sociology. Throughout this process, critics from within women's studies charged that feminist scholars were replicating the white male misconception that conflated Western traditions with all knowledge. Thus, Woman as a single category in feminist research receded and women with their multiple identities based on race, class, ethnicity, religion, age, ability, and sexual orientation began to emerge.[3]

As a result, the amount of new material in women's studies is nothing short of staggering. Yet, work that addresses itself to the question of delivering this information in the classroom is scarce. We must begin again to examine our early pedagogical commitments, this time in light of the expectations of 1990s women's studies students and their campus environment.[4]

The 1990s college-age cohort was born and raised in a world that provides multiple and conflicting messages about women. On the one hand, there is the message that "you can be anything you want to be," pervasive in college recruitment materials and in special programs designed to attract women to areas like math and science where they are underrepresented. On the other hand, American women live at risk of sexual abuse, rape, and domestic violence in a culture, both public and private, that, moreover, persists in conflating womanhood and motherhood. Women's studies offers a safe place to explore mixed reactions to these mixed messages. The 1970s foremothers to these students concentrated on securing enough power to guarantee a space, physical and intellectual, within the academy. The lesson we have learned is that securing the space does not resolve the power issues, it merely clarifies them as women students continue to push toward full recognition and acceptance of women's presence. The women's studies classroom is the students' opportunity (perhaps their only one) to experience and experiment with models of learning that begin in that full recognition and acceptance. Hence, the contributors herein write about the classroom as a site of praxis. They understand that knowledge is political and they understand that to promote change in their academic and social worlds is a political act.

This collection is not an exercise in analyzing students' writings—we take them at face value as comments on both the process of engaging feminist scholarship and pedagogy and as critique of higher education in general. Repeatedly, in the process of developing this manuscript, we have met with two opposing responses. Students who hear about the project are enthusiastic. They tell us that they rarely have the forum for discussing their willingness to learn or the obstacles they encounter. Faculty tend to respond to the project with doubt. What do students know about teaching? Could we find publishable writings? Were the insights original enough to warrant a book? Sure, there are a few good student papers every year, but enough for a worthwhile book? It is in this gap—between teachers' sense of students' abilities and students' sense of students' abilities—that the learning process is constructed. The value of this book lies in its ability to bridge that gap, to remind faculty to incorporate the needs of their students into classroom instruction.

All of the authors in *Engaging Feminism* wrote their contributions while undergraduate or graduate students at Duke University from 1986 to 1990. Duke is a private research university of some 11,000 graduate, undergraduate, and professional school students. At the collegiate level it is a residential college specializing in the liberal arts. At the graduate level it is a highly respected research institution that trains scholars. As a select school, it draws students from among the most academically talented and financially able cohorts in the country. Few students are beyond traditional college age; the percentage of minority students was 18.2 percent in 1990, slightly higher than the national average of 15.7 percent.[5] The Women's Studies Program is in its eighth year and offers an array of courses, degree concentrations, and campus activities, much as many other programs do.

As the director of Women's Studies since the program's inception and as editor of *Signs: Journal of Women in Culture and Society*, Jean has a long-standing interest in discovering more about the ways in which students interact with the subject matter of women's studies. That interest infused her conversations with colleagues, among whom Mary, then managing editor of *Signs*, held a special place. Having worked together on the journal while it was at Duke University, we shared a commitment to promoting the new scholarship on women and to integrating it into the classroom. With the rotation of *Signs* to another campus, Mary was free to pursue this interest more directly, first teaching a senior seminar in women's studies and then joining Jean in exploring the student writings.

Our thoughts began to take a more definite shape when Nancy Essig, director of the University Press of Virginia, visited Duke and met with us. We talked about our interest in understanding the women's studies enterprise from the students' points of view. We told her that we had read powerful and provocative writings by the students taking our classes, that they were publishable, but that, well, a collection of student writings about higher education had never, to our knowledge, been published. We considered whether there was enough material (yes, there was) and whether or not a university press would publish such a collection (yes, it would). With her encouragement, we were on our way.

We turned first to the program's archive of journals from a graduate seminar in the history of feminist thought. We read through four years of journals—literally thousands of pages of comments on readings, on speculations about what has been written by women, and, alternatively, on what had been canonized by men. In amongst the sentences about the course readings nested another kind of writing altogether—first-person narratives. These passages stood in sharp contrast to the passive and abstract way in which students recorded most of their ideas. We pulled out all of the personal narratives and set them aside for a closer look.

Then the questions surfaced, "Is this narrative style somehow a by-product of the graduate student experience, or do undergraduates use this style, too?" During 1989–90, we solicited work from undergraduates who had written journals, thought papers, or essays for courses sponsored by women's studies—including a capstone seminar for seniors in women's studies, the student-designed courses based in the residential units, and the introductory women's studies course. We found a similar division in the material. Most of it was written in standard academic prose, with the learner/writer a distant, objective commentator on the topic at hand. Sometimes there was a shift in tone and voice, however, and a narrator would emerge, speaking about how the course material connected to her (or his) personal experience. Although the undergraduates had different interests and skills than the graduate students, this phenomenon they shared in common. We selected a few especially apt examples of the "commentator" style and all of the first-person narratives and set them alongside our other stack.

With all of the extracts in front of us, we spent the summer reading them and then reading them again. We followed a methodology developed by sociolinguists for doing conversational analysis, in which a small group of researchers pore over the material repeatedly—discussing what it means, identifying patterns, and deciding how best to describe what they find. We were joined in this enterprise by an advanced graduate student in English, Mary Bowman. We met several times a week—trying out one organizational premise, discarding it, and trying another; trying one group of readings together and then another until coherent categories emerged.

We used nearly all of the material available to us (one piece dropped out because the author decided not to release it; another few pieces dropped away because they restated points made by others). The table of contents that thus evolved reflects a familiar concept in women's studies—a learning process that moves from individual emotional experience toward collective action. We have organized the writings to take the reader through a process of learning in women's studies that starts with its emotional impact (anger, frustration, resentment) and then moves to reconsidering familial relationships and friendships, learning about feminism, developing a feminist identity, assessing the classroom environment for women, learning about the campus environment (rape, sexual harassment, sexual relations, and sexual identity), and teaching and learning within the women's studies environment.

The book concludes with a collection of writings that practice a politics of knowledge, moving beyond critique and toward concrete and constructive action. They differ from those in preceding chapters in both purpose and voice. These three papers did not originate in course work but in activist efforts to improve the contributors' living and learning environments. We have included these longer pieces in order to document student-generated initiatives for change that have had institutional impact.

In short, we have organized the book to take the reader through the process of learning in much the same way that some students may have experienced it. Still, since each contribution is distinct (in terms of author, source, and topic) from those surrounding it, we cannot say (nor is it necessary to say) that these readings show students moving through the learning process in this particular order. Indeed, our point is that learners probably experience learning idiosyncratically, depending upon their inclinations and interests at the moment. The process recognizes a range of reactions, however, and the many points on the range reflect the multiple ways that students engage ideas in the women's studies classroom. A record of these moments of engagement appears here—a significant number of them from journals.

One distinguishing feature of women's studies since its earliest days in the 1970s is its use of journal writing.[6] However, even now, the purpose for which journals are kept; the nature of the entries; the question of whether they are read wholly, partially, or not at all by the instructor; as well as the parameters set for students' writing—all vary with each course, instructor, and institution. There is no accepted orthodoxy on journals as a pedagogical tool.

In the graduate seminar in the history of feminist thought from which many of these writings come, the journal is a part of the learning contract that structures students' work. Each student establishes an individual learning contract that builds relationships between the class readings and their disciplinary training. It is drafted by the student, discussed with the instructor, modified, and then shared with the entire class. Because an enormous amount of reading (over two hundred pages a week) is covered in the course, the students formulate a central question that serves as a guide through the readings. Questions typically explore the nature of and explanation for women's oppression, the relationship between emotion and reason in women's experience and interpretation of it, the role that education plays in women's lives, or the construction of women's sexuality. About half of the students redefine or switch their questions in the middle of the semester. That is, they begin reading to understand one topic and by midsemester find another one more interesting. Such changes are encouraged as long as the students are self-reflective about what they are doing and can reformulate the learning contract's bridge to their disciplinary work.

The journals then become the main vehicles by which students record the progress of their learning experience. No research paper is required in the course. The journals, leadership of some class sessions, general contributions to discussions, and a midterm and final oral exam constitute the basis for formal evaluation. The journals are meant to serve as a record, primarily for the student's future reference, of works read, ideas noted, and insights explored. They are collected several times throughout the semester for comment by the instructor. The length of journal entries varies by student, by week, and by topic. In general, the more time students spend working on their advanced degrees, the more they write in their journals—sometimes as many as fifteen pages a week. Students who are beginning their scholarly and professional training tend to write much less—sometimes as little as four pages a week. Thus, each student has her (or his) own goals for their journals. Some students write their journal entries after having read the material for class but before class discussion. Others use the journal to record their reactions to the classroom discussions of the readings. For students who had not used journals before, or for those who had kept journals for other purposes in other classes, the exercise itself challenges their assumptions about learning and scholarship. Karen B., for instance, in the journal extract that follows this introduction, expresses her uncertainties about her own journal writing.

In general, the journals we read recorded the students' reactions to the course readings, summaries of the works, and comments on the ideas, style, and stance of each author. As the semester progressed, the students wrote more comparatively, discussing the readings in the context of earlier readings, classroom discussions, and material from outside the course. The students were asked, specifically, to incorporate class discussions into their writing. They were not asked, or expected, to record personal experiences. Yet, as the semester passed, they became more likely to do so. Why that was so is a matter of speculation, of course, but we think the answer lies in the sense of self-worth that emerges in a feminist learning environment.

The contributors to *Engaging Feminism* have a great deal to say about learning processes and learning environments. Their thoughts are complicated, subtle, often eloquent expressions of frustration, tension, insight, intellectual commitment, and emotional entanglement. Each journal extract has its own rich history in the personal life of the student, but most

7

of the contributions included here share a narrative style (first person) and a focus on a moment, a turn in perspective—from the specific ideas presented in the classroom to ruminations about family, friends, society, culture, truth, silence, and self. None of the writings were written for the public, and we use all of them with the explicit permission of the authors. Many of the writings are so profoundly sensitive that the authors chose to use pseudonyms (Karen B., for example)—a choice that is itself a statement about the degree to which students feel silenced, alienated, and vulnerable.

Whether or not the contributors to *Engaging Feminism* are representative of women's studies students in general is hard to tell because national figures are unavailable. Among our sixty contributors, nine are women of color, five are men, and six are returning women students. There are forty-two graduate and eighteen undergraduate contributors. Whether they are representative in terms of these various social indicators or not, they are a diverse lot in terms of the points at which they intellectually engage knowledge and the ways in which they see that knowledge as meaningful. In this, these contributors are like students in other U.S. institutions of higher education, and so they have something to offer any self-reflective teacher, any disoriented and alienated student, any emerging feminist. Still, this book is not about the contributors but about what the contributors have to say. In this, they are among the first students to speak a critique of higher education in print.

As we worked with their writings, we were struck with how rarely the students wrote about themselves in the process of learning. What is it about the instructional process that removes the self from the analysis? What are the consequences of doing so? What prompted students to "go against the grain" and write in the first person? What did that tell us about what they were learning? We found ourselves wondering if the journal process somehow allowed first-person narrative, however seldom, in a way that essays or other writing exercises did not. Was it something special about women's studies or was it something special about the particular classroom environments at this particular university? We wondered how we might share the students' insights as a first step in exploring some of our questions. As we began to write, one thing became clear: universalizing statements about students had no place here. The contributors herein show us inner voices that speak with honesty, vulnerability, determination, and sometimes self-confidence. Read together, the voices are diverse, complicated, and unpredictable.

As we searched for companion literature to ground our arguments, we reread work by feminist scholars who developed the case for women's studies as a necessary new direction in higher education.[7] This work offers a sharp critique of the status quo in higher education, examining and exposing the ways in which implicit assumptions about women affect male faculty interactions with women students. Faculty can and do discourage women from asking questions or participating in discussions by not calling on them or by challenging them if they do speak up; they make casual, denigrating comments about women as they lecture; they omit materials by and about women from their syllabi; and they may sexually harass women students, offering good grades in exchange for sex.[8] The feminist critique of higher education is vital to improving the classroom environment for women, yet it is only one part of a still emerging agenda for necessary change. To end masculinist practices is not necessarily to engage feminist ones. We believe that the next step in feminist reconstructions of the academy is to challenge the authority relations of faculty (the class of knowers) to students (the recipients of knowledge) by developing a student-based critique of teaching and learning.

Though women's studies has emerged relatively recently, it is only one part of a longer history of women's struggles for access to higher education and their resistance to the confines of subordinate, domestic roles within it.[9] In the last two decades, the new scholarship on women has taken this effort to the level of content, exposing the ideological underpinnings of women's marginalization in the traditional, Western curriculum. It is a precondition of their experience, as it is recorded here, that today's women's studies students have access to both the classroom and the curriculum.

The contributions in *Engaging Feminism* reveal that many students in women's studies are keenly aware of both the limitations of the male-biased educational status quo and the tension-filled promise of feminist pedagogical practices. It is a tension-filled promise because, of necessity, feminists must incorporate the unlearning of the old dyads—living and learning, emotion and reason, community and individual, teacher and student, creator of knowledge and consumer of knowledge, powerful and powerless—into the search for more productive paradigms. Nancy Schneidewind and Frances Maher put it this way: "Changing the process of how we teach is often more difficult and risky than changing the content of what we teach." Moreover, "while it is convenient to imagine that one can simply incorporate the content of women's studies into the curriculum and present it to students in the traditional format, it is necessary to realize . . . that process and content are inextricably linked, that how we teach is inevitably linked to what students learn." [10]

In this way, then, feminist pedagogical practices sparked by the new scholarship on women—as experienced by the contributors to *Engaging Feminism*—challenge nothing less than the structuring assumptions of teacher/student relations in American higher education. When teachers assume that competition, isolation, and self-doubt are productive motivators (or teach as if they assume this), they subordinate their students' skills and talents to the idea that rewardable achievements preclude collaboration, cooperation, and trust. Such assumptions were honed by white male faculty on white male students; they do not helpfully address the more diverse interests and learning practices of peoples of color, women, or (for that matter) white men. [11]

The primary insight of *Engaging Feminism* is as simple as it is revolutionary. We believe that students are, in contributor Connie Pearcy's phrase, in the class of knowers. The writings included here attest to their knowledge and their ability to critique. We are convinced that their points of view are absent from the vast majority of discussions about American educational reform today, including but not limited to feminist critiques of higher education. These students' insights into the nature of their educational experiences can and should require all of us to reconsider our agendas for change. [12] So, although we share a concern with many others about how to improve the quality of American education, we work toward this goal from an uncommon direction. We offer for consideration students' critiques of their education. We offer an opportunity to listen—to listen to those who can teach us how to encourage the will to learn.

AS I START TO WRITE THIS JOURNAL

Karen B.

As I start to write this journal, I feel somewhat uncertain. I really haven't thought very deeply about what I hope to accomplish in this course besides simply becoming more familiar with the various strands of feminist thought. That's an important goal, of course, but it doesn't seem sufficient guidance for writing this journal, for trying to articulate a goal to direct future journal entries. I also feel a little timid in starting a new class, with a professor I haven't worked with before. After last semester's course I have certain habits and attitudes about journals—mostly I am tending to want to think about myself in the face of classroom readings, how they make me feel and why, what about them excites, encourages, discourages, dissatisfies, scares, infuriates me, and how my opinions and attitudes are beginning to alter in dialogue with these. But this is a different class—and though woman-centered and accepting of diversity, I wonder—will that approach seem "acceptable," seem sufficiently "scholarly"?

SEARCHING FOR AN AGENDA

Anne Chandler Scott

October—feeling terrible: My voice is tight—I'm not secure—people wait for what I have to say to be over—it was composed for another moment and now seems canned—I can't just jump in—I am some sort of observer, not affectionate or gregarious: Joey, a Mechanical Boy. There are certain people who speak with authority, from experience, and I'm not one of them. I'm not reading—I'm not thinking—I'm not talking—I'm writing but it doesn't mean anything. . . .

November—feeling somewhat better: I see myself putting on a shy persona and I want to avoid that. I feel people responding to it—trying to behave chivalrously—and this will do me no good. I'm embarrassed about the personal details I've shared; they seem to paint a picture of lifelong repression. Instead, I am striving for a picture of myself as simply accountable—as influenced by context and having some influence over consequences—and this seems to be as difficult on a personal level as it is on a movement-wide level. It is so hard not to relapse either into guilt or quietude—taking responsibility for everything or for nothing. . . .

December—I began this journal with the theme of "searching for an agenda." I was so self-conscious about not having one, and so uneasy about the paltry equipment I did have, that I felt it necessary to put my really important reflections in brackets. Incorporating them into regular prose, I knew, would be too paralyzing. At least I knew that much! But the true value of these reflections was something that had yet to be recognized by the very apparatus that had produced them. In other words (to get away from metaphors of mental hardware, and to move toward myself as a user of tools), I knew intellectually that I should draw from my own resources as a subjective knower—but I had yet to know this subjectively. . . .

The way I'm writing this reminds me that I want to be, and still am not, a

11

"constructed knower"—one who trusts the inner voice, adapts procedures and received ideas to specific contexts, and can work collaboratively. (Though the fact that I want to be one of these also reveals the extent to which perfectionism is still my philosophical guide.) But I have developed this social, other-directed part of myself, and that was exhilarating. I've done what I tried to describe earlier in my journal—made the circuitry of other-directedness more sophisticated, so that the energy also serves my own needs.

1. This is an idea many educational reform advocates have put forward over the years. See, e.g., Adrian Blunt, "Education, Learning and Development: Evolving Concepts," *Convergence* 21, no. 1 (1988): 37–54; Fred J. Dowaliby and Harry Schumer, "Teacher-Centered versus Student-Centered Mode of College Classroom Instruction as Related to Manifest Anxiety," *Journal of Educational Psychology* 64, no. 2 (1973): 125–32; Nancy E. Downing and Kristin L. Roush, "From Passive Acceptance to Active Commitment: A Model of Feminist Identity Development for Women," *The Counseling Psychologist* 13, no. 4 (October 1985): 695–709; Kenneth A. Feldman, "Effective College Teaching from the Students' and Faculty's Point of View: Matched or Mismatched Priorities?" *Research in Higher Education* 28, no. 4 (1988): 291–344; Zelda F. Gamson, "Changing the Meaning of Liberal Education," *Liberal Education* 75, no. 5 (November–December 1989): 10–11; Steven A. Massura and John F. Feldhusen, "Effective College Instruction: How Students See It," *College Student Journal* 12, no. 2, pt. 2 (Spring 1978): 1–12; Margaret A. McKenna, "Shaping the Change: The Need for a New Culture in Higher Education," in *Changing Education: Women as Radicals and Conservators*, ed. Joyce Antler and Sari Knopp Biklen (Albany: SUNY Press, 1990), 295–301, esp. 301; Mary Rose O'Reilly, "Exterminate . . . the Brutes—And Other Things That Go Wrong in Student-Centered Teaching," *College English* 51, no. 2 (February 1989): 142–46; Barrie Thorne, "Rethinking the Ways We Teach," in *Educating the Majority*, ed. Carol S. Pearson, Donna L. Shavlik, and Judith G. Touchton (New York: Collier Macmillan, 1989), 311–25. For an alternate viewpoint, see Walter C. Hobbs, "Academicians Are Not Gods, and Students Are Not Persons," *Journal of Higher Education* 39 (1968): 281–83.

2. See Deborah Silverton Rosenfelt's edited collection of writings by students, *Learning to Speak: Student Work*, published as *Female Studies*, vol. 10 (Old Westbury, N.Y.: Feminist Press, 1975).

3. The "Can we learn anything about women?" and "Is it important?" debates are closed for all but a few who think that the Western tradition's loss of status in the academy narrows rather than expands opportunities for educational reform. See Jerry Adler et al., "Taking Offense," *Newsweek*, December 24, 1990, 48–54; Allan Bloom, *The Closing of the American Mind* (New York: Simon and

Schuster, 1987); Dinesh D'Souza, "Illiberal Education," *Atlantic Monthly* (March 1991), 51–79; and Fred Siegel, "The Cult of Multiculturalism," *The New Republic*, February 18, 1991, 34–44.

4. Some scholars have explored women's ways of knowing as influenced specifically by gender norms. This work, by implication, suggests that gender norms may influence differences in problem-solving approaches and learning processes, as well. See Mary Field Belenky, Blythe McVicker Clinchy, Nancy Rule Goldberger, and Jill Maltuck Tarule, *Women's Ways of Knowing: The Development of Self, Voice, and Mind* (New York: Basic Books, 1986); Carol Gilligan, Nona P. Lyons, and Trudy J. Hanmer, eds., *Making Connections: The Relational Worlds of Adolescent Girls at Emma Willard School* (Cambridge, Mass.: Harvard University Press, 1990); Nancy E. Downing and Kristin L. Roush, "From Passive Acceptance to Active Commitment: A Model of Feminist Identity Development for Women," *Counseling Psychologist* 13, no. 4 (October 1985): 695–709; Blythe Clinchy, "On Critical Thinking and Connected Knowing," *Liberal Education* 75, no. 5 (November–December 1989): 14–19; and Jill Maltuck Tarule, "Voices of Returning Women: Ways of Knowing," *New Directions in Continuing Education* 39 (Fall 1988): 19–33. For studies that focus on differences between men and women, see Catherine G. Krupnick, "Women and Men in the Classroom: Inequality and Its Remedies," *On Teaching and Learning: The Journal of the Harvard-Danforth Center* 1, no. 1 (1985): 18–25; Frances Maher, "Pedagogies for the Gender-Balanced Classroom," *Journal of Thought* 20, no. 3 (Fall 1985): 48–64; and Susan L. Gabriel and Isaiah Smithson, eds., *Gender in the Classroom* (Urbana, Ill.: University of Illinois Press, 1990).

5. Alexander Astin, *The American Freshman* (Los Angeles: Higher Education Research Institute / University of California, 1990).

6. See *Female Studies*, vols. 1–10, for an early attempt to begin defining the discipline. This journal compiled syllabi, program descriptions, bibliographies, and essays on feminist pedagogy in which there were frequent references to journal keeping. There are also a few articles dedicated to the topic. In addition to Rosenfelt, ed., *Learning to Speak* (*Female Studies*, vol. 10), see Ellen Berry and Elizabeth Black, "The Integrative Learning Journal," *Women's Studies Quarterly* 15, no. 3/4 (Fall/Winter 1987): 59–64; T. Fulwiler, "Journals across the Disciplines," *English Journal* 14, no. 9 (1980): 14–19; and Phyllis A. Walden, "A Learning Journal as a Tool to Promote Lifelong Learning Skills," *Feminist Teacher* 3, no. 2 (Summer 1988): 14–17, 35.

7. On the academic discipline of women's studies, see Antler and Biklen, eds., *Changing Education*; Gloria Bowles and Renate Duelli Klein, eds., *Theories of Women's Studies* (Boston: Routledge and Kegan Paul, 1983); Marilyn Boxer, "For and About Women: The Theory and Practice of Women's Studies in the United States," *Signs: Journal of Women in Culture and Society* 7, no. 3 (Spring 1982): 661–95; Ellen DuBois, Gail Kelly, Elizabeth Kennedy, Carolyn

Korsmeyer, and Lillian Robinson, *Feminist Scholarship: Kindling in the Groves of Academe* (Urbana, Ill.: University of Illinois Press, 1985); Florence Howe, *Myths of Coeducation* (Bloomington: Indiana University Press, 1984); Elizabeth Langland and Walter Gove, *A Feminist Perspective in the Academy: The Difference It Makes* (Chicago: University of Chicago Press, 1981); Frances A. Maher, "Toward a Richer Theory of Feminist Pedagogy: A Comparison of 'Liberation' and 'Gender' Models for Teaching and Learning," *Journal of Education* 169 (1987): 91–100; Helen Roberts, ed., *Doing Feminist Research* (Boston: Routledge and Kegan Paul, 1981); Julia Sherman and Evelyn Beck, eds., *The Prism of Sex: Essays in the Sociology of Knowledge* (Madison: University of Wisconsin Press, 1979); Dale Spender, ed., *Men's Studies Modified: The Impact of Feminism on the Academic Disciplines* (New York: Pergamon, 1981); Liz Stanley and Sue Wise, *Breaking Out: Feminist Consciousness and Feminist Research* (Boston: Routledge and Kegan Paul, 1983); Catherine Stimpson, *Women's Studies in the United States* (New York: Ford Foundation, 1986); Paula Treichler, Cheris Kramarae, and Beth Stafford, eds., *For Alma Mater: Theory and Practice in Feminist Scholarship* (Urbana, Ill.: University of Illinois Press, 1985).

On women's studies as a curriculum transformation project, see Susan Hardy Aiken, Karen Anderson, Myra Dinnerstein, Judy Nolte Lensink, and Patricia MacCorquodale, eds., *Changing Our Minds: Feminist Transformations of Knowledge* (Albany, N.Y.: SUNY Press, 1988); Sandra Coyner, "The Ideas of Mainstreaming: Women's Studies and the Disciplines," *Frontiers* 8, no. 3 (1986): 87–95; Margo Culley and Catherine Portuges, eds., *Gendered Subjects: The Dynamics of Feminist Teaching* (Boston: Routledge and Kegan Paul, 1985); Linda Dittmar, "Inclusionary Practices: The Politics of Syllabus Design," *Journal of Thought* 20, no. 3 (Fall 1985): 37–47; Margot C. Finn, "Incorporating Perspectives on Women into the Undergraduate Curriculum: A Ford Foundation Workshop," *Women's Studies Quarterly* 13, no. 2 (Summer 1985): 15–17; Diane Fowlkes and Charlotte McClure, eds., *Feminist Visions: Toward a Transformation of the Liberal Arts Curriculum* (University, Ala.: University of Alabama Press, 1984); JoAnn Fritsche, ed., *Toward Excellence and Equity: The Scholarship on Women as a Catalyst for Change in the University* (Orono, Maine: University of Maine—Orono, 1985); Pearson, Shavlik, and Touchton, eds., *Educating the Majority*; Marilyn Schuster and Susan Van Dyne, eds., *Women's Place in the Academy: Transforming the Liberal Arts Curriculum* (Totowa, N.J.: Rowman and Allanheld, 1985); Karen J. Warren, "Rewriting the Future: The Feminist Challenge to the Malestream Curriculum," *Feminist Teacher* 4, no. 2/3 (Fall 1989): 46–52.

8. This point is made by Montana Katz and Veronica Vieland in their student-directed book, *Get Smart! A Woman's Guide to Equality on Campus* (New York: The Feminist Press, 1988), 39: "Student-professor relationships are a key element of college education. They can offer lessons to the student on nonacademic subjects, too. Relationships with male professors can serve to instruct the female

student in maintaining a subordinate status within the college community." For a survey of the research on this topic at the primary, secondary, and postsecondary levels, see Myra Sadker and David Sadker, "Confronting Sexism in the College Classroom," in *Gender in the Classroom*, ed. Gabriel and Smithson.

9. Sally Schwager, "Educating Women in America," *Signs* 12, no. 2 (Winter 1987): 333–72, esp. 365–69, 372.

10. Nancy Schneidewind and Frances Maher, eds., "Feminist Pedagogy," a special issue of *Women's Studies Quarterly*—vol. 15, no. 3/4 (1987): 4; Kumiko Fujimura-Fanselow, "Feminist Pedagogy: Its Goals, Principles and Implementation," *Toyo Eiwa Journal of the Humanities and Social Sciences*, no. 1 (1989), 95–113.

11. For work that explores the implications of content changes for teacher/student relations (as they are seen from faculty perspectives), see Elsa Barkley Brown, "African-American Women's Quilting: A Framework for Conceptualizing and Teaching African-American Women's History," *Signs* 14, no. 4 (Summer 1989): 921–29; Elizabeth Ellsworth, "Why Doesn't This Feel Empowering? Working through the Repressive Myths of Critical Pedagogy," *Harvard Educational Review* 59, no. 3 (August 1989): 297–324; Elizabeth Higginbotham, "Designing an Inclusive Curriculum: Bringing All Women into the Core," *Women's Studies Quarterly* 18, no. 1/2 (Spring/Summer 1990): 7–23; Ruth Nadelhaft, "Predictable Storm in the Feminist Classroom," in Fritsche, ed., *Toward Excellence*, 247–56; Paula Rothenberg, "Integrating the Study of Race, Gender, and Class: Some Preliminary Observations," *Feminist Teacher* 3, no. 3 (Fall/Winter 1988): 37–42; and Schneidewind and Maher, eds., "Feminist Pedagogy."

12. For a first-person account of a teacher's struggle to maintain her own desire to learn, see Nancy Porter, "Liberating Teaching," *Women's Studies Quarterly* 10, no. 4 (Winter 1982): 19–24.

ONE

Reasoning with Emotion

There is an oral tradition in women's studies that says that emotions go with the territory: if you teach women's studies you are going to have to deal with the unexpected, the folk wisdom says. Teachers of women's studies trade stories—of resistance to the idea of studying women, of tears when the classroom discussion comes very close to home, of stormy silences when classroom issues are long-denied personal ones, of outbursts when one student turns to another and says, "Why am I only now learning about women? Why didn't I know this stuff?" There are long talks after class that try to connect all that is being named to all that is being felt. If you take a women's studies course, so the campus grapevine goes, you will have a series of experiences—experiences of feeling both anger and elation, of having some friends find you strange while others seek you out; experiences that cause you to doubt both what you have usually done and what you are now doing; experiences of getting a small glimpse of the lives of your teachers and wanting to know more while at the same time thinking that your teachers do not have personal lives. Students and teachers in women's studies know they feel as much about the subject as they think about it. Yet the written wisdom on the women's studies enterprise mentions little of this.[1]

Sometimes students encounter the new scholarship through experience with and information about sexism and discrimination, sometimes through discussions of feminist activism, sometimes through studies of patriarchy,

16

or women's history or women's literature. Whatever the spark, the anger is an important aspect of their motivation for learning. At the same time, even while some students' energies are fueled by this confrontation, other students struggle with confronting the self-doubts—the corrosive effects of sexism on self-esteem—or with the complicated ramifications for understanding the world in which they live, turning the assurances of the taken-for-granted into anxiety and guilt. Lucy Edwards explains that she has spent the seven years since her emergence from a fundamentalist religious cult trying to understand "the outside world. . . . Comes the feminist critique of that outside world, and I am truly filled with anxiety."

The confusion that surrounds and compounds these emotions is the inheritance of a tradition that tells us that learning is a rational process. Most traditional classrooms operate on the assumption that reason is the surest route to knowledge and the only pathway to thinking. The new scholarship on women, sexism, and discrimination has promoted the erosion of this exclusive assumption because it is an assumption that silences and alienates students, and it distorts both the knowledge and the learning of it. Indeed, the traditional collaboration between power and reason requires students to be receivers of knowledge and empowers faculty to be the producers of knowledge. As a result, emotion seems to have no place in the learning process. The lie, of course, is that the emotions are there, they happen anyway; in women's studies classrooms they can be acknowledged and validated.

We begin this book on feminist learning with contributions about these emotions not only because the teaching of women's studies requires their recognition but also, perhaps more important, because they are so central to the students' learning process. As Johnnella Butler says, "Feelings are direct lines to better thinking. The intuitive as well as the rational is part of the process of moving from the familiar to the unfamiliar in acquiring knowledge."[2]

OPEN NEW DOORS

Liz Morgan

If feminism is going to help, it must open new doors, not just oil the squeaky hinges on the old ones.

CHANGING THE RULES

Judith W. Dorminey

Changing the rules is different from just fixing the system so that there is a place for women. Changing the rules is different from women taking the responsibility for entering the economic and political world and functioning there as full human beings. Changing the rules is a threat and a danger and a radical thing and probably the only thing that is going to make a difference in how the world works.

THE CLASS OF KNOWERS

Connie E. Pearcy

Assertions invite question/examination—facts demand respect/belief. . . .

Fact: Science is a powerful tool in the hands of great men.

Fact: The truth is that Einstein was brilliant.

Fact: Men and women get intoxicated from different amounts of alcohol because they have different levels of an alcohol-processing stomach enzyme.

Assertion: Science seems to be a powerful tool in the hands of great men. (What kind of tool? Why were all these men great? Why were they all men? What does great mean? What did they do?)

Assertion: I believe that Einstein was brilliant. (Why? What did he do? What does brilliant mean? Should I care?)

Assertion: After studying a number of women and men, we found that, as a general rule, men can drink more than women before getting intoxicated, and that these men had more of an alcohol-processing stomach enzyme than the women. (How many people were studied? What other factors besides this enzyme are involved with intoxication? How much more alcohol could the men drink and how much more enzyme do they have? What factors besides sex affect enzyme levels? Why study women and men?)

To say something is true defies the notion of the scientific method in action—we don't know the truth, we can only approximate it. Yet "Truth" carries with it the power of "Science" and vice versa. Since science must be reserved for those who are trained to be scientists, who speak the language, who know all the facts, the lay folks must trust researchers to reveal the truth and to inform us of their findings. Science is revered and removed from daily life and placed in the lab. Life experiences become irrelevant when searching for the "truth" and are even potential distractions. We no longer view knowledge of all kinds as experiential at all levels. Some experiments have become more valid and valuable than others. Some people have become the class of knowers while others must be the recipients of knowledge.

WHY AM I SO ANGRY?

Kerith Cohen

Question: "A friend says to you, 'Sexism just doesn't really exist anymore. Modern women can do whatever they want to. Discrimination against women doesn't happen any longer.' How would you respond?"

Answer: If I can do whatever I want, then why am I terrified when I walk to the Bio-Sci building every Sunday evening for my sorority meeting? How many men wander up and down their halls, looking for someone to walk them to their cars after dark? And how many men would be blamed or called "stupid" or "asking for it" if they couldn't find someone to walk with and were attacked on the way to the parking lot?

If I can do whatever I want, then how could men in my first-year dorm leave their doors unlocked and prop the fire-escape doors while women were attacked in the stairwells and bathrooms? And why was the solution locking the women's bathroom door and not the fire-escape doors?

If sexism just doesn't really exist anymore, then why can I not watch a Duke basketball game on TV without seeing barely clad bimbos in every beer commercial? Why are cars and alcohol marketed as tickets to fulfilling men's fantasies: acquiring numerous, young, buxom women (girls) to decorate their automobiles or serve them beer?

If discrimination against women just doesn't happen anymore, then why are only 2 percent of people in Congress female? And why am I, by virtue of my anatomy, denied freedoms which every day men take for granted—going to the record library on East Campus any time it's open, and not only before dark; selecting my clothing by what *I feel like* wearing, and not what may be interpreted as provocative; inviting an acquaintance (Duke student or not!) into my room to talk; the unquestioned ability to control my own body.

If sexism really doesn't exist any longer, then why, when I go to the movies, is the "ideal" couple portrayed by Richard Gere, who is probably forty-five years old, and Julia Roberts, who is probably twenty-two? If men become distinguished as they age (Robert Redford, Sean Connery . . .) but women are only desirable if they are young, is this double standard not sexist? And if sexism doesn't exist, then why am I told I am overreacting or being silly if I point this double standard out to my friends as we leave the theater?

If economic discrimination against women doesn't happen any longer, then how do you account for the study which has proven that women with generous financial resources are less likely to marry? And that the best chance a poor, divorced mother has of improving her economic status is through remarriage?

If women can do whatever they want to, then why is "women's work," housework and child rearing, still done by women—maids and daycare workers—when upper-class women have careers? And why is this work still devalued, seen as "acts of love," not as work? And when these services are paid for—why are zoo attendants paid more than child care workers?

If sexism doesn't exist anymore, then why am I so angry?

I THOUGHT MY MISERY WAS PERSONAL

Judith W. Dorminey

Oh, wow! It's a good thing I didn't read Sara Evan's book when it was written. Not that I would have had time. I had a three-year-old, a six-year-old, a husband just starting a new career, a budget dead from two years of business school, a soul dead from coping with seven years as new mom/military wife, and a body exhausted from doing everything for every body except mine. I simply did not have the physical or emotional energy to pay the slightest attention to the women's movement. I thought my misery was personal and had I known that others felt as I did, my rage would have been without limit. I might have walked out on the whole enterprise and missed what I have discovered and grown in a different way. As it is, the retrospective rage I feel is barely containable.

PATRIARCHY IS A PERFECT CIRCLE

Kat Turner

It never fails to amaze me what a beautiful setup patriarchy is, a perfect circle that is extremely tough to break. Men establish that they are superior, and they convince women of this fact. They take the most powerful jobs and highest pay, they take emotionally without giving, they are catered to and humored—and they claim that this is their due because they are inherently more capable. Then, because they are in positions of power, they do research that supports their claims to superiority and natural dominance, they pass laws to ensure that they retain their lofty positions, and they control the media that informs the public about this. They have successfully brainwashed women into accepting their lower positions. And women buy it! (Obviously not all women.) Although the system sickens and depresses me, I have to give it to men for their utter ingenuity and wile. I couldn't have thought up a more self-serving society if I tried!

WHAT IF THEY'RE RIGHT?

Kathryn West

Sometimes, even after all the reading I've done in women's studies and otherwise, all the discussions I've had, all the theoretical and economic and historical analyses I've read and heard, sometimes I still feel like "But why? What happened?" Have you ever felt that sometime, somewhere, some undiscovered thing must have happened that caused women to be so feared, so hated? As if there were some sort of conspiracy. And sometimes it all gets so bad, and there are so many examples of inequities and hatreds directed at women, that something really insidious creeps in and just for a second you wonder, "What if they're right? What if women really are lesser creatures?"

HIDE AND SEEK

Anne Chandler Scott

The position of having to react, and having to examine one's reactions, is an uncomfortable one. I back away from the difficulty of the emotional work that is necessary to become visible, proud, and allied. Hide-and-seek is easier: hiding my own specialness (about which I have profound doubts—both in the area of "smartness" and in the area of ethnic/class/sexual identity), and seeking alleviation for my guilt from those whom the "mainstream" has excluded. I shrink from the attitude of defiance which, I tell myself, would be an easier way into solidarity. Is it going to be this difficult to be authentic? How can I stop myself from feeling aggrieved when a group regards me as "other"? How can I stop myself from evading conflicts, smoothing differences away with the selective impulse toward inclusion-because-we-say-so that my middle-class, liberal background has trained me in, almost as a form of etiquette? How can I get away from being merely nice?

STRUGGLING WITH A FUNDAMENTALIST PICTURE

Lucy Edwards

When I was eleven years old—as old as my younger son is now—I was reading the literature of the fundamentalist religious cult that I eventually joined (privately, by dint of personal decision) when I was fourteen years old—as old as my older son is now. . . . Coming from a small midwestern town and a working-class family with virtually *no* concept of critical thinking or of history or literature or philosophy or *any* part of our received, Western cultural past, and going into this fundamentalist sect as young as I did . . . my conceptual world has been defined in most significant ways by the worldview of the cult. But when I was twenty-nine I was born again. That is to say, I was kicked out of the cult. I do not exaggerate or engage in metaphor when I say that on the day I was disfellowshipped, the ground moved beneath my feet when I walked. I cannot begin to describe the emptiness, the total lack of moorings and meanings that I knew on that day, and for many days to come.

On December 10 of this year, I will have been out of that cult for seven and a half years. I am now physically, emotionally, and—especially—

conceptually in a place that I could not even have conceived of less than a decade ago. I have spent most of these seven years trying to understand the world "as it is," though I realize the dangerous ambiguities inherent in that phrase. I have needed to understand our cultural orthodoxy so that I could take up my life again and live "in the world." The universe that feminists are questioning and taking apart, however, is the universe of that "mainstream" world to which I have returned so recently and with such checkered success. Even after seven years, I continue to find that I lack conceptual categories that others around me take for granted and use without thinking; therefore, I often find myself struggling not only to follow the line of some argument that's being presented, but to ferret out the implicit categories that are being used to present the argument. I am still struggling with a fundamentalist picture of the "outside world of thought." Comes the feminist critique of that outside world, and I am truly filled with anxiety.

GUILT

Charles Paine

How about *Guilt*. I've realized for quite sometime that, all other things being equal, had I been a woman I most likely would never have graduated from college. I have a lot of personality traits that are, in our culture, characteristically female, but they have been less damaging, less powerful in holding me back, and the reason they are less powerful is because I have the benefit of being a man. In other words, I realize that in addition to growing up middle class and white, I've had the immense privilege of being male to thank for my doing anything with my life. How do you deal with being an oppressor, with having reaped the rewards of being born privileged? It seems to me that guilt can work the same way anger does— as a motivator, an impulse to right the wrongs of centuries upon centuries.

I've recollected (sometimes with considerable pain) several previously unremembered memories. Usually the memory was of an experience in which the principal emotions were shame and humiliation. The three main ones all had to do with older boys chastising me for not conforming to acceptable young-man behavior. I suppose one reason that feminist concerns make so much sense to me and seem so important to me is that I've been aware (unconsciously at least) of the pernicious influence that gender rigidity has had on my own psyche. I don't have much analysis to

23

offer here, except that such rigidity of roles may not be the *source* of much of the sadness and confusion I felt growing up and still feel now, but it has made things harder to figure out. Again, I still have trouble with proposing myself as a generalizable subject, but I've become more cognizant of how culture constructs us, often in a way that goes against our grains. It's easy to blame something outside of ourselves for our sadness.

DOMESTIC CHORES

Deborah K. Chappel

When I think about the many meanings "domestic" has assumed, it's no wonder we're so anxious to escape its stigma. A domestic is a low-paid household worker, cleaning up others' messes in houses which don't belong to her. Domestic wine is cheaper and used for the everyday meal instead of the special occasion. Domestic animals are tame, grown on farms to be slaughtered for their meat or raised in kennels to be kept as pets. Domestic chores are those which just need to be done again. . . .

I can understand our desire to distance ourselves from tasks and a private sphere which has consistently constrained and demeaned us, but *somebody has to change the sheets and wash the dishes*. Period. There has to be some way to think about domesticity which doesn't link it so firmly to exploiting women.

The domestic chores I do around the house are those which most contribute to my physical comfort and the well-being of those I love. We look at work in the public sphere as so important, but its effects are so diffuse too. My real life is affected so much more directly by having my house clean, my clothes laundered, healthy dinners on the table, than it is by real estate salesmen, auto workers, and business managers. I benefit directly from what's done in the public sphere, I know, but it doesn't seem to affect my life as immediately or as much as having that private sphere be clean, orderly, and harmonious. I'm having to personally cope with liking a clean house and clean clothes but feeling guilty for the time spent on these things, because that time takes away from my *real* work as a graduate student.

I'M NOT FEELING GOOD

Alice Nelson

I've been working for thirteen hours a day on the computer for the last five days. I type extremely slowly, granted, but the real problem is sustaining the excitement of the gains and the frustration, anger of the setbacks of centuries upon centuries of feminism. Another good reason to work on a journal, and to do it gradually. This marathon has been emotionally, psychologically, and physically intense. My stamina in all respects is hovering at about zero right now. Something had to give, and it was, most obviously, my body; I've got some fluish bug that's gone from nasty cough to fever to vomiting. I'm not feeling good, but I've also gotten a bit depressed about what I'm doing: both the situation I've created and the material are depressing me. Never before have I been driven to tears by my work. It's not that I don't have the desire; on the contrary, it's because I'm deeply invested that I'm reacting so strongly. I need to back off emotionally from the texts, and to get some sleep, so I'm gonna print this out and go home.

I'm glad I figured out what was going on with me, and that I can do something about it. I'm learning a lot here.

THE LOST VOICES OF WOMEN

Kathy Rudy

I spent this morning reading meeting notes and journal entries from the Divinity School Women's Center—10–15 years ago. I am so frustrated! The things they were talking about are *exactly* the same as now . . . inclusive language, inclusive language for God, women faculty. The lost voices of women at Divinity School haunt me.

Had lunch with ———. She says not to talk to her about it because it makes her feel hopeless. The cycle is there . . . there is nothing we can do about it. It's "built into" Christian theology. If we say that sexism or whatever it is that keeps the cycle of forgetting going is or is related to original sin—no way to stay Christian (how can a *male* savior save women?). Who will work this out?

And spending the evening reading about women's history since the En-

25

lightenment—how much more can I take? Each time I am confronted with someone who has been erased from history . . . I feel as if someone is hitting me on the head with a brick. It's not that I mourn for or with that person, because her woman's voice is lost—no, I cry out in pain because I see no other alternative for my own life than to eventually be lost or erased. All the work I have done and hope to do will someday be as obscure. And there's nothing I can do.

Each time the brick is about to hit my head I scream (to patriarchy)— how can you do this again? Where is your compassion? Your sense of ethics? Stop!!!

But something (something very little and unsupported) seems to be rising from the pain in my head . . . yes . . . *how can* you do this???? There must be a million tiny little things that are allowing my sister's voice to be deleted. (Eye contact in the classroom, "If God is male, male is God.") *I want to learn them all*—then live as if they didn't exist.

1. For two exceptions, see JoAnn M. Fritsche, "Why and How to Assess Student Responses to Curriculum Integration," in *Toward Excellence and Equity: The Scholarship on Women as a Catalyst for Change in the University*, ed. JoAnn M. Fritsche (Orono, Maine: University of Maine—Orono, 1985), 158–63, esp. 159; and Lynn Weber Canon, "Fostering Positive Race, Class, and Gender Dynamics in the Classroom," *Women's Studies Quarterly* 18, no. 1/2 (Spring/Summer 1990), 126–44.

There is also discussion of angry resistance to women's studies courses: see, e.g., Christina L. Baker, "Through the Eye of the Storm: Feminism in the Classroom," 224–34, and Ruth Nadelhaft, "Predictable Storm in the Feminist Classroom," 247–56, both in *Toward Excellence*, ed. Fritsche; and Elizabeth Higginbotham, "Designing an Inclusive Curriculum: Bringing All Women into the Core," *Women's Studies Quarterly* 18, no. 1/2 (Spring/Summer 1990): 7–23.

Some authors have concentrated on the emotions generated by competition among students in the classroom: see, e.g., Cheris Kramarae and Paula A. Treichler, "Power Relationships in the Classroom," in *Gender in the Classroom*, ed. Susan L. Gabriel and Isaiah Smithson (Urbana, Ill.: University of Illinois Press, 1990).

Our focus, however, is on the experience of absorbing new information in learning about women, sexism, and discrimination. For a review of feminist teaching practice vis-à-vis this focus, see Renate D. Klein, "The Dynamics of the Women's Studies Classroom: A Review Essay of the Teaching Practice of Women's Studies in Higher Education," *Women's Studies International Forum* 10, no. 2 (1987): 187–206. Klein indicates that students' views of their experiences have yet to be made public (188) and concludes with a call for attention to "the complex multifaceted tensions arising from the mismatches between the dreams and the realities" of women's studies students (201).

2. Johnnella Butler, "Transforming the Curriculum: Teaching about Women of Color," in *Multicultural Education: Issues and Perspectives*, ed. James A. Banks and Cherry A. McGee Banks (Boston: Allyn and Bacon, 1989), 145–63, esp. 154.

TWO

Exploring Relationships

The demographics of contemporary American families make generalizations about The Family impossible. The emotional ties that most of us have to the people we love and those who love us in those families are deeply important to our self-image, our sense of community, and our ability to develop new friendships. Likewise, the institutions of the larger society that support the traditional nuclear family as well as the forces that foster other family structures play an important role in the ways we think about ourselves, our families, and our friends.

Many women's studies courses touch on various aspects of these inter-relationships between family, society, and culture. Material, for instance, about the American labor force, or ideologies of race and class, or theories of psychological development can lead to classroom discussions of family and friendship as structural influences on the individual as well as provoke personal reflections outside the classroom. This process of reexamining one's family and community as a part of shaping a growing sense of self is a particularly complicated enterprise for many of those taking women's studies. The complications arise from the fact that the process and the intellectual framework are at once the subject and a critical perspective.

When a student learns that women's work in the home has been under-valued economically, it is an essential part of the learning process that this student consider her (or his) own context for assumptions about women's work in the home. Learning about this historical reality causes the student to reflect on her relationships with female family members. When a student learns about concepts like economic dependence, class divisions, differences in women's traditional roles, the gender- and race-related division of emotional and economic labor, the cultural constructions of family (and the cultural differences between families), the apparent contradiction in Western culture between "femininity" and "intellectual," or the importance of female friendship, she is learning about something she has already experienced, something she knows by example. That something now has a new meaning given the information presented in her women's studies class.

Incorporating classroom understandings into open understandings among family and friends is another matter. The fact that four of the fourteen contributors in this chapter chose to use pseudonyms suggests that it may be a difficult, sometimes impossible, task to explain these new perspectives to others. One returning woman student, Judy Dorminey, in "While the Family Has Slept," writes of the ways in which her family and community have responded to her new priorities. About her dreams she says even her husband, her best friend, "doesn't know it all." Yet seeing oneself in the context of a community has its rewards. As Kim Dowell puts it, "We need each other for support and for the rich experiences one gets from knowing and intermingling with diverse black women."

The journal extracts that follow testify to the depth and distance that these explorations take students—from mother to father and siblings, to husband and community, to friends and lovers.

I'VE ALWAYS LIKED DISCUSSION

Claire O'Barr

When I first encountered the idea that objectivity isn't a given in science—and particularly in the social sciences—I was excited. That may seem strange. I have never felt comfortable with science and I never liked that it had "right" answers. I've always liked discussion. So, lately I have been both puzzled and bothered by people's acceptance of and unwillingness to question "facts." . . . In the past couple of years I have discussed this with several friends—one engineering student in particular—who simply could not understand, much less deal with the idea that a "fact" is not a universal truth, and that maybe there are no "universal truths." I find this troublesome, particularly in reference to the many, many changes and false ideas that science and the world have had and reinterpreted over the past five hundred years. I have trouble understanding people's views of the world which leave no room for change and reinterpretation. I see things much more on a continuum—of which we are a part.

LINES THAT DIVIDE BLACK WOMEN

Kim Dowell

There are many lines that divide black women. Such things are sexuality, politics, shade of skin, class, and nationality. I think that many women do not realize how their prejudices toward other black women affect each other. Black women need to unite—we need each other for support and for the rich experiences one gets from knowing and intermingling with diverse black women.

To begin with, sexuality and politics divide black women. . . . Just as homosexuals are discriminated against by society, so are lesbians by women. Also, some black women are treated with disdain because they choose to date or marry someone of another race. Because of this, it does not mean that these women have betrayed their race. Black women should not be penalized by other black women because of their sexual orientation, choices of mates, and the politics behind their choices.

Also, black women are looked down upon because of the shade of their skin. . . . Darker skinned women are viewed as not being as attractive as lighter skinned black women. This is a problem that has survived through the years. Black women come in all different shades of colors—just like the rainbow, they are all beautiful.

Furthermore, class and nationality seem to divide. . . . I feel the recognition of one's nationality is fine as long as it is realized that all blacks in America are seen as a collective group and that they need to band together to survive and excel. Also, . . . the elite blacks do not have much personal contact with lower class blacks or middle-class blacks. They may help the black masses from a distance, but they need to come and relate with black people of all classes. If not, they will lose their culture and heritage and even their blackness if they are not careful.

MY MOTHER IS AMAZING!

Barbara G. Heggie

In singing my mother's praises, I often chant a litany: My mother is amazing. She does everything. She teaches learning disabled children in the high school, she leads the student international club, she sings in the church choir, she teaches Sunday school, she leads the 4-H group, she's the president of the local Association for Retarded Citizens, she's on the board of directors of the local United Way, she's a member of the Ambulance Corp, she's on the board of directors for Literacy Volunteers, she makes breakfast, lunch, and dinner every day from scratch, she bakes bread every Saturday morning, she does all the cleaning in the house, and she sends me care packages of (you guessed it) homemade cookies. Don't you *dare* criticize her!

Of course I do anyway. I wonder what kind of society makes this woman feel that she has to do all this in order to be happy, and I vow never to do the same. What makes my mother not want to join the AAUW because "they only do things for themselves"?

THE BOND THAT BLACK WOMEN SHARE

Marie E. Nelson

Black womanhood is not monolithic, instead its expressions are diverse extensions of individual passions that should be respected if not accepted. Whether a sister chooses to become a lesbian or feels that to be happy she needs a man, neither needs to attack the other. It's hard enough dealing with what the rest of society has to throw out in our way; for us to demean one another just seems so self-defeating.

There are so many beautiful parts of the bond that black women share— the nurturing, the strong sense of religion, that undeniable sense of "style," the love and kinship from our extended families, and these are the things that we must covet and protect because this is what keeps us fighting back. Without the love for ourselves and our sisters, survival in today's society is made moot. After all for what is it that we live?

IT'S A MATTER OF PRIORITIES

Jane R.

I "saw" the women's rights movement through my mother's eyes, so to speak. My mother tended to see herself as someone that the women's rights movement didn't "speak to," and so I tend to see her that way as well, or at least recognize that that is how she sees herself. Insofar as you respect your mother, you don't want to totally embrace a movement that she feels excludes her. Now you might say that she shouldn't have felt excluded, and should have raised her consciousness, but it gets complicated. I still have difficulty with this issue, because I have always been sympathetic to "women's rights" and feminist claims. But my mother has not. I guess she's sort of antifeminist. But what is hard for me is that since my father has always undervalued her and the fact that she is the emotional backbone of our family, it's like my being a "feminist" is a slap in the face and rejects everything she values. And since what she values is not valued by my father, in particular, I don't want to reinforce the belief that what she has done is less important than "what men do" or what I plan to do.

My mother did a lot of volunteer work. She may have been motivated, in part, by a desire to get out of the house and to find validation, but quite often there are religious motivations for doing such work, for believing that you have social obligation to the less fortunate. And we weren't wealthy— lower-to-middle-class—when I was growing up. Many volunteers in small towns in upstate New York were not wealthy women with lots of time on their hands, but women who felt an obligation to help others. Now there may be all sorts of reasons as to why women, as opposed to men, feel obligated in this way, or why the Church is able to use women in these capacities. But when discussing the motivation of volunteer women, we often have to look at the religious and ethical motivations, for many women are quite sincere in their efforts and do not see volunteer work as a mere panacea or replacement for "real work."

I'll admit, and I think that she would admit now, that my mother was in part escaping from being trapped within the problems of my family, which were not inconsiderable when I was growing up. But motivations are never clear-cut, and I think there was a genuine desire on her part to help other people. In addition, my mother represented someone who could understand so many things my father (an attorney) could not understand, so I always felt as though her priorities and values should not be devalued.

Last year, my mother got a job for the Hunger Action Network of New York State, and the reason she was hired was because of all the volunteer work she had done and because of her experience in dealing with these sorts of issues. She didn't have any kind of degree (two years of college and then married). If the state had its priorities straight they would have officially put someone in her present position years ago. . . . My point is just that it's a matter of priorities, and quite often women feel that certain things are important even though no one else is willing to do them, such as coordinating food pantries and soup kitchens.

REBELLION

Alice Nelson

My brother and I were kids in the sixties; my oldest brother was off at college in Tennessee and my sister was a teenager (my parents were in their forties). We were growing up in rural southwest Virginia. . . . My oldest brother and sister represent a baseline of "child of the fifties," and while "rebellion" only indirectly intersected with my brother's life, my sister became somewhat politicized in her last two years of high school (but then she got married, but that's another story). My brother and I were too young to participate but plenty old enough to observe (as time has gone on, we're the most politicized of the four). What's most interesting to me is how radically differently my sister and I grew up. She was a trailblazer for me in more ways than one (now our roles might be reversed, but I'm not sure). She was more than thoroughly indoctrinated in the "rules of femininity" by my parents (mandatory ballet lessons serve as a symbol here), who doled out approval to her for being "pretty," for performing in "feminine" sorts of ways, etc., and either didn't notice she was smart or (non?)verbally undercut any sense of achievement she could realistically expect to derive from this or other sorts of skills she had. She rebelled; fights ensued over issues as varied as activism, sex, and marijuana. My sister got pregnant, didn't have an abortion (you can tell who "won" that one), got married (my father said, "Be a schoolteacher," and so it was), got divorced (and is now a remarried yuppie with her own business and mother of three; needless to say, she ain't a total revolutionary, but I learn/ learned a lot from her). For me, the symbolic ballet lessons were scrapped (they actually came up, but I refused, and they accepted it, but the point is that gender expectations were a lot different for me and my brother than they were for my sister—and than they were for my older brother). I didn't get the same sorts of messages from my parents that my sister had. Sure I got the marriage spiel (and I still get it), but the sorts of (gender) expectations and limits communicated to my sister were minimum for me by comparison, and dialogue was opened up on issues of sexuality, my decisions on all sorts of matters respected, etc. By the time my adolescence rolled around in the mid-seventies, a lot had changed. Bear in mind that my parents still relentlessly ridiculed my sister, for example, for voting for McGovern, but social change had happened on such a broad scale that it had penetrated our conservative rural southern community and our home. All things considered, we had come a long way.

MY PARENTS SEPARATED

John D.

My parents separated three years ago. It was an amicable separation—they simply no longer (if they ever actually did) loved one another enough to overcome the lack of intimacy and spiritual emptiness. Two years ago, my parents began drawing up the lines of settlement. Remarkably, even this went rather smoothly—money can't buy happiness, but it sure helps one escape from unhappiness. Anyway, the point I'm trying to illuminate revolves around my mother's demand (too strong) for 60 or 70 percent of their combined assets. She showed me the divorce counselor's memo with my Mom's figures juxtaposed with my Dad's. My emotional reaction was that my Mom was being greedy. At the time, 50 percent even seemed a little unfair to my father, who, after all, had worked hard for thirty years to achieve his high salary. What had my Mom done but raise three kids? Now don't get me wrong: I appreciate the amount of physical and psychic energy involved in child rearing, but the quality and quantity of my mother's care did not increase when my father started bringing home the big bucks and we had a big house and Volvos.

That was precisely my line of thinking two years ago. My mother argued that in 1962 women gave up their jobs at Time, Inc. and their half of the partnership became housekeeping and child rearing. She felt that she had done her part commendably (who am I to argue?) and so, with the bargain (contract) being terminated, her investment in time and energy had come due.

Retrospectively, the terms of their contract were mutually unfair. My mother was not rewarded for her good work and my father was punished for his. Under the circumstances, it was resolved in the fairest way: my Mom got most of the liquid assets and my Dad took his six-figure salary to the West Coast and the incipient stock-market crash.

My mother now has *a room of her own* (an eight-room house, actually), financial independence, and relative security. She is also getting a Master's degree at age fifty-one. It would have all been much simpler and more equal had she pursued her career from the get-go.

MATERNAL AUTHORITY

Wendy Wagner

I think about how my mother and her sisters have bonded together since my grandmother's death ten years ago and how that void of maternal authority led them to seek relationships among themselves. In addition, I have begun to think that their increased dependence upon each other is also a reaction against my grandfather who always seems to exist in a shadowy borderline of involvement in my mother's and aunts' lives, having remarried soon after my grandmother's death. What do I mean by reaction? I mean that they either repudiated or responded to the lack of paternal authority as well. . . . I thought that nothing could ever break the bonds that had developed between my mother and her sisters. They had shared, given each other so much in terms of spiritual, emotional, and material support. But since my grandfather died last May, my aunts have rejected "sisterhood" and replaced it with a reverence for the father; those members of the family who do not attempt to fulfill my grandfather's wishes are excluded from the "family." After his death my grandfather is more powerful and authoritative than he ever was in life.

I AVOIDED INTIMACY

Steven T.

I am a very closed person by nature and for a long period of time I have closed my emotions and my feelings off to the outside world. When you fail to think about or talk about emotions for a long period of time, their importance is greatly diminished. I remember myself as being a very emotional person up until about high school. Over the years since then, I have pretty much detached myself completely from my emotions. This detachment was reinforced by my father. While my mother is a very emotional person, my father has always been an even-tempered man, his only outlet for feeling being an occasional outburst of anger, usually justifiable. He deeply loves, cares for, and most of all respects my mother, but I believe that he views her as being of a very different species than he is, one with inherent flaws.

I am not going to criticize my father—he is a remarkable man who most likely would have been among the "enlightened" himself had he been born forty years later. I am going to criticize myself. I believe myself to be a very emotional person. Unfortunately, I have no idea as to the nature of these emotions. I have subconsciously modeled myself in my perceived image of my father—an honorable and hardworking man capable of withholding a great deal of feeling from the outside world. I have denied myself some of life's greatest sufferings and joys because of the path I have taken. There are few things in life that make me very sad. I have been able to detach myself from most death and suffering. However, I rarely go through the ecstatic periods of joy or love that I seem to remember being capable of at some point.

It is very difficult for me to deal with people on a very intimate basis. In the past, I felt as if it was because my feelings and thoughts were very different from everyone else's, and to open up to someone would not only seem to present me as being weak, but also as a bit of a bore. So I remained close-lipped about my feelings and avoided intimacy.

I no longer buy into that argument. I have reached a point where I would like to open my life to another person. However, I have forgotten how. I am not capable of discerning my own emotions. Last week, I was forced to call an old girlfriend to ask her how I should deal with a new one. In a matter of minutes, she was able to tell me what I was feeling inside. I was not so much shocked by the fact that she knew—she knows me better than most. What surprised me is that I did not know.

GOOD MOTHER/BAD MOTHER

Mary-Mallette Acker

In the past, I feel as though I have avoided thinking very much about the mother-child relationship because I don't have any children and I'm not sure that I ever will. Distancing myself from this sort of discussion has proved very comfortable for me. I convinced myself that I couldn't possibly relate to anything connected with motherhood, and I've even been a little resentful that so much of the literature deals with women as mothers. My own relationship with my mother is really very good, and I don't feel like I've experienced many of the problems that most women describe in their relationships with their mothers.

. . . The conflicts between being a *good* mother and a *bad* mother can be transferred into other personal relationships as well. . . . The same split . . . is evident in a woman who works and is involved in an interpersonal relationship. She has to feel torn between her work and her relationship at certain times. Also, I can foresee a similar split in myself in the event my parents become dependent on me in later life.

What I don't understand is why men don't experience this internal split similar to the way women do. I'm convinced that most men seldom experience any father-child split. There may be a more significant split in men when the issue of dependent parents arises, but even that would probably be less intense than the feelings of women. This suggests to me that a lot of the worrying and concern about being *good* versus *bad* is due to socialization. Men, in general, aren't expected to worry as much about making a relationship work, so they don't experience the split. Women, on the other hand, are expected to nurture the relationship (or child); therefore, they often find themselves *placed* in the middle by having society's expectations forced on them.

I find this whole discussion . . . to be problematic. It would appear to me to be more productive to discuss the connections between mother, child, and work than to focus on separating the three. The very fact that a woman is a mother is going to influence her being in the world, and she will necessarily draw from her personal experiences as a mother. I think this notion of splitting is unrealistic. I don't believe it's possible to objectively dissect individuals' feelings and actions and to explain why they are the way they are.

GIVE US MORE RESPECT

Michelle Beaty

When I first had a man tell me that black women are disrespectful to black men, I thought he had lost his mind. After all, haven't we loved, supported, and been there for them? They're the ones who ought to give us more respect, I thought. . . . But I've begun to consider my attitudes as manifested in my actions toward men. I don't trust them and, because of that, I don't expect much from them. Most of the males in my family have contributed to that attitude. Surprisingly (to me anyway), my mother and aunts have also done their part to perpetuate the idea of black men as "passing through." It's not that they always physically leave, but, even when they stay, they do not have any real power within the family structure. I wonder to what extent this has affected my ability to enter a relationship with an open mind.

WHILE THE FAMILY HAS SLEPT

Judith W. Dorminey

It took me forty-seven years to struggle through the two centuries from Bays Mountain, Tennessee, through the birth and rearing of three children, through the isolation of being a traditional wife and hausfrau to get to graduate school. For the last three years I've driven almost forty thousand miles and eight hundred hours between Charlotte and Durham (a statistic derived along the lonely stretch between Archdale and the Yadkin River on I-85) and never missed a paper and rarely a class. I've studied while the family has slept; I've read assignments while waiting in grocery lines and at soccer games; I've planned papers while my hands cooked hot meals, folded laundry, and scrubbed toilets; and no one has missed an ironed shirt or a kissed hurt or a tumble in bed. I have spent my inheritance in advance and forfeited any prospects of "Three Guineas." Now I am within sight of a Master's degree with a certificate in Women's Studies.

The people at the university seem to think that I'm an aging housewife who makes good grades because she "doesn't work" and has plenty of time to study. The people at home think I go to graduate school to give myself something to do when I get bored with dabbling in domesticity. My parents think my rich husband is indulging my whim and wonder why I haven't invested their generous preinheritance gift or used it to redecorate the house or take the family on a long trip. I haven't even told my best friend the whole dream. He knows I want to write and he knows I want to stay close to a college and the ideas that float around a campus, but even he doesn't know it all.

BEST FRIEND

Juanita J.

I had a best friend from whom I was inseparable—she left the country when I turned twelve (I saw her again briefly when I was fifteen, then twenty-one) and I remember sobbing for a week after. I couldn't eat. I felt a part of me had been wrenched away. And looking back, I think a part had. I have tried to recover that intimacy with female friends, and I think I have succeeded to some extent. But now there isn't that unqualified/ unlimited devotion—Maria for me meant everything. She came first, no matter what, as I did for her. Now I am more wary, more cynical, more conscious that for most women, chances are their lovers/husbands will come first, that girlfriends are important, but that ultimately, it's your *family* (the one you're working toward), your *man* that comes first. And as a *friend* (my mother, father, culture tells me), I just have to accept that. It's what I've been taught, and what I (unfortunately?) have come to be-lieve, to some degree. Because I think—whether or not I'm committed to developing strong bonds with women—the social and cultural conditions in which I live will force the women with whom I come in contact, and myself, to make these choices, to choose men/family over female bonding. And I think that it's this "consciousness" that precludes the kind of trust, the utter faith I experienced when I was twelve.

I was also thinking that I still look for that. I want to rediscover/re-construct the intimacy of that friendship with Maria, in my heterosexual relationships. And I don't think it's possible, simply because of the way I was brought up—differently, apart from men, with different notions of what "love" entails (gendered spheres/expectations/training). Men have different ideas about what intimacy means, what a sexual relationship en-tails/demands, what expectations I, as a woman, may have that do not coincide with my lover's. It's an area in my current relationship that needs work. And yet, I have been thinking lately that maybe it's foolish of me to want that much from it. That I can have different people—men and women—play different roles in my life, fulfill different emotional needs. That maybe one person *can't* be everything (and that one person never *was*, even though I remember her as such) and that it is unfair/deluded of me to ask anyone to fulfill me in such a complete and totalizing way. That maybe I shouldn't require that total understanding from my boy-friend and instead should accept what my relationship with him can give me. That intimacy does not hinge on *total* understanding—that perhaps it means recognizing the gaps in our understanding of each other, and caring enough for each other to respect and appreciate that space, as well as to work inside it/with it.

And yet, something rebels inside me at the thought, and I think, no, it's not enough, and, no, dammit, I want more and I'm not willing to settle for less. And again, I wonder how much this desire is tangled in the fairy tale dream/ideology of a Prince Charming who will be everything I ever dreamed. I mean, is this desire of mine simply a fantasy that cannot come true, period, or that cannot come true at least in our culturally determined space? It's what my boyfriend argues when we talk about my doubts, my insecurities. And still, I think, there's something wrong with this relationship—if I look elsewhere, maybe I'll find that person who can make me relive that first love. And still, again, I find myself thinking how stupid it is of me to believe in that first love (so blindly?), as though it was everything I remember it being.

I've been conditioned to look for it (a reenactment) in men, been told that in this society only the man with whom I form a family will never leave me, will love me unconditionally—that friends will always have other priorities. And yet, I feel from experience that it's the other way around— that it's the men who usually disappear and abandon their wives and children, and that it's the women relatives/friends who would never dream of such a betrayal. Of course this is all complicated, and I'm making huge generalizations, and there will be men who won't leave, and there will be women who will compete more than love, who will betray, stab me in the back for a man (imagine that!). But still, I live with these (fairy tale?) notions in my head. And they seem like such foreign elements when I search them out in this light.

WE DENIED OUR SISTERHOOD

Donna M. Thompson

As a black student, the pressure to be better and brighter than everyone else was constant and intense. It began with the president's freshman address in which I was told that I was the future of my country and ended with our forging out to rule the world after graduation. On the other hand, women at Yale also felt a loss of femininity. Realize that we were the other factor in the infamous tradition of male road trips. Granted this wasn't a problem before 1970, but once women were admitted to Yale road trips took on a completely different meaning. Nearly every weekend some group of men drove off to meet the woman of their dreams or at least of the moment at Smith, Mount Holyoke, or Albertus Magnus. We at Yale decided, indeed were told, that men made these ventures because Yale women were unfeminine, too intellectual, too much like them to be considered as mates. Insecurities piled up on top of insecurities. So to beat the system we played along with all their jokes. Chuckled gleefully at the less than subtle innuendo that accompanied any discussion of the "women's colleges." Conversations ran like this—"Smith to bed, Holyoke to wed"; "Hey guys there's a party tonight at Albertus Mattress"; "My sister didn't do too hot on her SAT's so she's gonna go to Smith." We walked an uneasy path between being taken as prudish intellectuals or as stupid bimbos. We denied our sisterhood for a date to the parties after the Yale/Harvard game.

THREE

Engaging Feminism

One of the most empowering aspects of the new scholarship on women is its grounding assumption that the absence of information about women in the classroom tacitly reinforces rigid gender role norms that silence women students. When those norms themselves become the subject of discussion, what was previously unspoken, unspeakable, becomes meaningful. What the unspoken means and whether or how well it can be expressed are, for everyone learning about feminist perspectives, individual struggles—sometimes shared in class or with friends, sometimes shared only in a journal entry. The hardest lesson to learn may be that feminism is not a list of ideological imperatives—it is a perspective with as many variations as there are people who call themselves feminist. It is not only a body of knowledge—it is a perspective on the process of building knowledge. It is not a training program in how to dominate men. It is a perspective on the subordination of women.

Having learned the lessons of exclusion and recovered the right to have a perspective and nurture it, those who embrace feminist ideas may find themselves engaged in a new struggle. As people who attempt to make a place for women in the world, to describe our experiences as grounding, feminists are in conflict with the dominant worldview. As Simone de Beauvoir said, "Representation of the world . . . is the work of men: they describe it from their own point of view, which they confuse with the absolute truth."[1] As a consequence, feminists must also confront those who would deny that women-centered approaches are useful or valid. Feminist perspectives, in other words, may be discredited for their challenges.

Feminists make demands, they want everything to be different, they are threatening. In such a worldview, feminists live with an image problem: we are seen as women who try to tell people what to think and then make them feel guilty for not agreeing with us in the first place. Though the contributors to *Engaging Feminism* are students who, by and large, have already discovered that feminism is something else altogether from its popular image, the writings in this section record ambivalences of "guilt by association."

This confrontation between negative images of feminism and positive, affirming experiences of learning about feminist perspectives is the theme that is common in the readings in this section. Some of the contributors are searching for a way to voice, to express, what they think—they are not so much resistant as they are unsure. Kathryn Firmin feels she would have to ignore her Catholic schooling in order to pass "certain litmus tests." Others seem disappointed with themselves or with feminism for not living up to standard. Deborah Chappel, for example, describes an encounter with a young bulimic student that prompts her to question her definition of a feminist. Still other contributors explore—sometimes with ambivalence, sometimes with confidence—how feminist perspectives have complicated and enriched their lives. Sandra N. writes about being accused of "ruining everybody's fun," and Colleen Seguin describes her attempt to help a woman "save face in front of her kids" as a feminist act. Most profoundly, moments in the readings are stark reminders that learning about the cultural invisibility of women can have deeply personal and individual impact. Donna Thompson explains how she encouraged her mother to read black feminist theory. "Her initial response was that she did not realize that many of the problems that she had struggled against growing up in Alabama had been feminist issues." As Eileen Anderson puts it, "By identifying myself as a feminist I feel that I can put my face where a blank might have been before."

BLACK WOMANHOOD

Erin L. Gibson

One issue that I have not clearly defined in my mind is the issue of my black womanhood. What does it mean to be a black woman? Do I really understand? Sometimes I just wish a fairy godmother would come tap me with a magic wand and say, "Now you contain all the qualities of a beautiful black woman." These qualities would be strength, love, support, and the gift of giving. I want to be able to find these qualities in myself. This is the kind of black woman that I strive to be.

A HORRIBLE DREAM

Karla G. Shargent

I had a horrible dream the other night. One of those which, when you wake up, it takes a few moments before you realize that it didn't actually happen. In my dream someone tried to rape me. It was at night, and we were outside. Fairly close by a party was going on. I struggled a lot, trying to get close enough to where the party was so that someone would hear my cries for help. I also made a conscious effort to remember enough of the features of his face so that I could recall them once it was all over and the effort to find and try him began. Well, I did get away, so it was only an "attempted rape." But I had a harder time remembering what he looked like than I thought I would. It had been so dark, you see. But then, right before I woke up, I realized what the real problem was. It had not been a man who had tried to rape me, but a woman.

As soon as I awoke and started to think about it, I realized that the dream symbolized some of the very real, but mostly unconscious, fears I still have about women's studies courses. I'm afraid of being *intellectually* "raped" by women who will try to turn me into a radical feminist. This, of course, is totally illogical . . . but so many of our fears are. Nothing like that has actually happened in class, or in my meetings with the faculty, but the worries and fears are there anyway. I'm not even sure what can be done about them except to continue going to class and learning to accept more and more that my fears are unfounded.

CALLING MYSELF A FEMINIST

Kathryn Firmin

I have always hesitated to call myself a feminist. I am increasingly persuaded that the epistemological/methodological framework women's studies scholars work out of is intellectually honest. The stance refuses to accept any knowledge as given or concrete; it instead queries how that knowledge was generated, what purpose it serves, and what questions were overlooked/ignored/hidden during the process of knowledge-creation. Further, I am quite willing to admit that women's history has systematically been erased from public view.

So what's my block in calling myself feminist? . . . I think feminists get so caught up in predetermined conclusions about the existence or cause of patriarchy that we can't look at alternate explanations for our condition. . . . Maybe I just had a bad experience; but I feel like the feminist scholars I've encountered have established certain litmus tests that I must pass . . . especially the prochoice movement, which I frankly have serious problems with—it's hard to ignore ten years of Catholic schooling, and I'm not sure I want to.

THE BLACK ELITE

April Conner

My goals in life lead me to be in the group of the black elite, or at least near it. Now, if and when I do attain my financial goals, I plan on behaving differently from the current elite.

It is difficult for me to *fully* comprehend why members of the black elite donate to colleges anonymously and perform other philanthropic deeds without making themselves known. Now, yes I do understand their stance that if white people know that you are rich, they (most likely) will try to destroy your wealth. I *know* that that happens. But still, to me, that just isn't enough to force people to do all their deeds anonymously.

To me, the entire purpose of achieving financial success is to be better able to serve my people, as well as myself. Therefore, I plan on being very public and *open about those things that I will do.*

FINDING ALTERNATIVES TO OPPRESSION

Patrick Inman

The effort to reach and be touched by "the other" must seem natural or expected in a man trying to learn from feminists, but it is equally necessary for feminists trying to learn from each other across ethnic, religious, class, national, and experiential boundaries.

What I am looking for in feminist thought are ways of thinking not only to identify oppression, but to express alternatives to it. . . . We must not only be able to identify oppression, we must be able to live ever freer of it in our own lives, becoming less and less victims and less and less exploiters. Beyond that, we must be able to communicate with, understand, try to change, learn from, and live with or fight those who do not share our understandings. . . . We need to see models of women developing and using new intellectual and social tools if we are to create alternatives that are inclusive.

WHO IS A FEMINIST?

Deborah K. Chappel

I've thought a great deal about how there isn't such a firm line between someone who is a feminist and someone who is not. This is very inchoate and tough to explain, but what I mean is that for many years before I became a feminist (the first time I called myself a feminist was a momentous event for me, like the first time I called myself a woman, as opposed to a girl), I had a lot of feminist ideas. Some were repressed, granted, and I certainly felt a great deal of anger that I couldn't admit. But it still seemed later that even when I was a secretary and a wife and didn't want more than that from life, what I am now was there, so that becoming a feminist was more like a gradual decision to be up-front about what I felt than it was some radical shift in my life. And looking back on conversations I've had with other women, both before and since I started calling myself a feminist, I recognized myself in women who said they oppose feminism. I had a student last semester who came into my office to discuss a paper, and while I was just beginning to call her attention to the assumptions that were floating around somewhere behind her rather fuzzy argument, she broke out in tears. She started talking about how everything that semester was asking her to question everything, and she talked a little bit about feminism, the essays she'd been reading in my class and others, and about how threatening these issues are for her. As it turns out, she's bulimic, extremely bright, very confused because she wants the whole wife and mother bit but more than that, too—she's just like all of us, I think. Maybe she'll call herself a feminist someday, or maybe she'll find some other way of dealing with her very real pain. But this made me think about what makes a woman a feminist. Surely there's pain involved there some-

46

where, since it seems like pain is always associated with women (with menstruation, with childbirth, with everything). If having suffered as a result of patriarchy is a prerequisite for feminists, this girl meets that test. If it's some kind of fellow-feeling for other women, I know plenty of women who call themselves feminist who lack that emotion. So I wondered about calling myself a feminist, and not calling her one.

THE POLITICAL ASPECTS OF FEMINISM

Mary Armstrong

When I began to explore what the political aspects of feminism might be, I was honestly rather uncomfortable with the topic. I thought about abandoning it, but I'm glad I didn't. At first I spent most of my energy trying to capture what political meant; it proved to be an elusive animal. I felt like I was chasing the Proteus Political—every time I had my hands on it, it turned into something different. Toward the end, I stopped being so worried about defining and looked more toward finding the common characteristics of the thought/writings I tended to consider political. Things went along smoothly then: the political indicated action, or change, or acting outside a system *or* the exact opposite, the decision not to act. In short, I found that nearly everything had a political dimension. Patriarchal or antipatriarchal, "public" or "private," most things seem to carry *some* political charge.

Since I felt less compelled to pin down the political exactly, I was free to try to find out where/why/how it showed up. Thus I discovered political agendas I hadn't noticed before. Because I didn't try to pin the political down, *it* didn't pin *me* down.

My goal of somehow harnessing the political modified itself into trying to discover where the political . . . fits into feminism and how feminism can best be political. I am convinced that a conscious approach to the political aspects of every action (or nonaction) is crucial for feminists. It is easy to expect too much of feminism. I think it was wise that I stopped praising or blaming aspects of the political and for the most part learned to concentrate on what it can and cannot do.

PRIORITIZING RACE

Donna M. Thompson

My mother under my influence has taken up reading black feminist theory. Her initial response was that she did not realize that many of the problems that she had struggled against growing up in Alabama had been feminist issues. They had always been viewed as racial issues. Differences in goals and life-styles tended to compel black women to choose between their race and their sex. Equality became the means to acquire a livable life. Perhaps equality was more of a necessity for blacks, whereas white feminists could approach it from a more theoretical perspective. Black women found it necessary to place race first because they were striving to aid their entire communities rather than to improve their own individual status in society. This prioritizing of race also created problems for black women. While white feminists simplify their struggle as one against "men," black women had to fight against the racism of the society at large. In their quest to overcome the inequalities of race they ignored the sexism of their own communities. Any attack against black men was seen as an attack on the race. Liberation could not be had on both fronts simultaneously. Unity was demanded by black men although this itself was oppressive to black women. It was a no-win situation for black women.

WHAT A WOMAN OUGHT TO BE

Miriam Shadis

I just remembered my first considerations of feminism. It must have been when I was in high school or maybe even junior high. I had this idea that feminists were constructing this idea of what a woman ought to be—what I ought to be—and I wanted no part of it. It seemed to me to be just another formula for people. As confused as it's been, my notion of myself has always been very strong—and very selfish. I wanted to be completely independent, and in that sense, completely unidentifiable. I think this is why I have a hard time even now with certain notions of feminism. I'm not as worried these days about identifying myself with any group—I've gone to the other end of not caring what other people think. But I still resent the kind of pressure I feel sometimes to discard parts of myself. So I still quote Emma Goldman: If I can't dance, I don't want to be in your revolution.

LOOKING FOR A CRUTCH?

Barbara G. Heggie

I often look to feminism and feminist theory to help me explain my own actions and pain and to give me a way to shift some of the blame for my hardships away from myself. . . . When I find exact replicas in only a few spots and close-but-not-quite-perfect reflections in most of the rest of it, I tend to think, "Oh, then it's just me." I realize I'm looking for a crutch.

Now I don't think crutches are bad. I think that one of feminism's most important functions for individual women is that of the crutch. Just so long as we don't become dependent on it, the crutch can allow us to mend our legs and learn how to walk on our own again.

BATTLING AGAINST ONESELF

Charles Paine

I've recently recognized that feminism has an especially bad reputation. . . . I'm realizing this when I examine my own reasons for avoiding women's studies courses until now and when I examine others' reactions to my telling them I'm taking a course in feminist thought. My father-in-law, for instance: he's a stock-market capitalist through and through, a hard-nosed believer in the land of good and plenty, etc.—*but* he doesn't mind my radical views of politics. But then I told him I'm taking this seminar, and he became genuinely concerned about my mental health—I mean, it really disturbed him, and it's the first thing he asks about when he calls these days. He really fears feminists, and he believes they are all "shrill," complaining about everything. And my father-in-law isn't alone. In the university (every one I've been to), just about every male had heard horror stories about men being "castrated" by "hard-core" feminists. Men have a tendency to fear feminists and feminism.

Now I'm absolutely *not* saying feminist thinkers should be passive, motherly-like stroking men: "There, there, we don't want your power." Yes, anger is important. But just about every male growing up in the United States has had the experience of being a patriarchal oppressor, holding oppressive beliefs, values, convictions, or condoning/forgiving oppressive attitudes. In other words, every male holds some *guilt*—and guilt is difficult (especially, I would think, for men) to deal with. I'm simply saying that it's hard enough for a man to get from guilt to nonpatri-

49

archal attitudes to taking action; people don't like to think of themselves as oppressors, and the cognitive dissonance will lead them to all sorts of strange convolutions of belief. I don't know what I'm trying to say: I guess it's that when you're trying to change someone's beliefs, you have to be firm but gentle—actually, I'd even say you have to be a bit crafty, a bit manipulative.

In a patriarchal culture, it's difficult for most men to completely rid themselves of all the conscious and unconscious patriarchal assumptions that affect their thoughts—it's a lot like "playing your parents' tapes," as they say nowadays: a boy gets his ideas about what being a man is from his father, and his ideas about relationships from both parents, and they probably were not exactly egalitarian in their views. In short, for the pro-feminist man, there is also the "battle against oneself": being self-aware, recognizing biases, trying to bypass the guilt, and changing assumptions. Personally, I don't think it's easy.

RUINING EVERYBODY'S FUN

Sandra N.

I have lately run up against the objection, presented with fear and sadness, that feminists want to ruin "everybody's fun" and destroy all that is beautiful about living and being a human being. Obviously, this sort of reaction is based on the fear of loss—of losing what currently gives life its meaning to some. I try to explain that, first of all, we are not trying to ruin *everybody's* fun, although if feminist changes took place, then, yes, *some* people would have their "fun" ruined. But their "fun" is fun at the expense of someone else. For example, if feminists can bring about some of the changes in society that they would like to, then we are going to ruin the fraternity boys' fun when "fun" is getting freshmen women drunk and "training" them at fraternity parties; and we will ruin the fun of the hooters and honkers who regularly harass women when they are walking or running on the street and on campus. And so on. But the world could use less of that kind of "fun." Men see the prospect of a more feminist world as dull, boring, and restrictive, I think, because for so long excitement and amusement and freedom have been for them and usually at the expense of others, because in some sense they know that it means sacrifice. The same way that integration meant sacrifice. Now, of course, they do not want to sacrifice the privileges that they have. And maybe the privilege to have fun, however it is that you do it, at whomever's expense, is one that they hold very dear. I'm reminded of how deeply committed people are to assumptions about the nature of men and women when they respond that feminists are dull, dreary, and bleak (among other things). And I think it's connected to the presence of women in business, in higher education, and in many traditionally male areas, where men not only have to deal with the presence of women in places they think women don't really "belong," but then they have to be careful of the jokes they tell and the remarks they make, and I'm sure it feels restrictive. But I can't feel too bad about putting a "damper" on things.

FEMINISM IN THE CHECKOUT LINE

Colleen M. Seguin

I am learning to live with the fact that I cannot be a politically correct Superwoman. I can't study, someday teach, be married, have kids, have time for myself, and be really active in the protesting/organizing/working aspects of the "real world" feminist movement, too. I also don't want to. I simply don't enjoy all of those roles and am not good at several of them. Besides, "consciousness raising" need not be strident or stereotypically "political." The most "political" I ever felt was not in a take-back-the-night march or an antipornography vigil (although those "genres" are very positive experiences for me). It was when a woman with whom I cashiered at the A&P came through my grocery line and ran out of money to pay for her order. The most painful thing that I have ever seen was for her to go over that order and eliminate things that she and her kids didn't really need that week. It was not solely that she ran out of money. It was also because I knew from working with her that she could not do math; thus when arriving at the register, she had no idea what her total would be (she was drastically over). Without going into all the details, suffice it to say that I totally messed up the balance in my drawer because of how I dealt with her returns. . . . Anyway, my point is not that she was a good, oppressed Everywoman and I tried to "save" her (she's not and I didn't)— it's that trying to help her save face as a mother in front of her kids and as a woman mattered at least a little for ten minutes or so and was in some way a feminist act.

WE'RE LIVING TIME LINES

Deborah K. Chappel

I grew up in the 1960s with 1950s values. The main impact the sixties had on me growing up, I think, was to frighten me and make me insecure.

This really came home to me when I read about the 1977 NOW convention in Houston. I was there! And yet, of course, I wasn't. I parked my car in the garage under the convention center, and I remember walking down the street and being stopped by some woman who asked me if I knew that I was oppressed. And of course I was. I was a secretary, in a miserable and confining (and miserably confining) marriage. But I remember that her question frightened me, like the pictures of police dogs and hoses and masses of marching, rioting people. This made me think about time. The 1960s movement happened for me as a time of turmoil, of me feeling the era's attempt to pull me from family and traditional values. I reacted to the era by clinging more firmly to family and traditional values. At one level. At another level, I was holding it inside, and the movement (at least, its goals and rhetoric) happened for me again after I came here. It's sort of like the time I spent in marriage, in a secretarial job, in Arkansas, even, was like the 1950s for me, when cracks appeared in the mold. When I became a feminist after coming to Duke, I think I was following the trajectory of these women in Sara Evan's book [*Personal Politics*] in a lot of ways. I think part of the problem of talking about "feminism" or "the movement" is that it's a kind of historical pattern that keeps repeating itself in waves over a much longer period of time. It didn't just happen in the 1960s. Just like saying that feminism has outgrown oppression, etc., when maybe some feminists have outgrown it (or think they have), but people just coming into feminism are moving in a different historical dimension. They're in the 1989 culture but at a different place in the development of feminism. The history of feminism, it seems, has to repeat itself in each of us. We're living time lines.

LESSONS FROM A SELF-DEFENSE CLASS

Patricia N.

My own engagement with feminism is rooted in the sixties kind of consciousness-raising groups—only mine happened within the university, in the 80s, and focused on Issues in Self-defense for Women. The strength, the sense of validation, shared experiences, willingness to listen, to talk, which I found in that group affirmed my loyalty to women's studies, and to women in general. If anything, that group experience destroyed most of my presumptions about what "feminism" signified (assumptions I had carried over/inherited from my mother, from the media, from school, which suggested that feminism was the favorite pastime of man-haters); it allowed me to create/understand feminism in my own terms, and feel that beyond my unique/isolated/individual conception, there was a shared space/ground that made me a part of a community. My notions regarding women— largely stereotypical, formed in accordance with dominant/cultural/male notions of what women should be, what they were and what they were not—changed; I began to find them beautiful and infinitely more interesting than the men I came across. This became something of a joke among my best friends at Stanford—all women—and myself; we all agreed that most men lacked brains and were incapable of interesting conversations/ insights. The women we knew, on the other hand, were fascinating. Time spent with women was much more fulfilling than time spent with men. This excluded, of course, our various heterosexual relationships—our respective lovers were our lovers because they had somehow escaped that socialization process, or broken through the gender roles, that otherwise inhibited communications between the sexes. I still think that this is, in some ways, true, although I would not be so crude these days as to dismiss one half of the human race as simply boring. . . . I think that many of my own biases against men at this time emerged from a new and radical empathy with women's experiences *as women*. Men were boring because I had nothing to say to them, nothing to share. Their concerns were not mine.

WE ALL NEED TO MEET MARY

Kathy Rudy

In a sense, I was raised, or raised myself, as a "feminist." I was born by the pen of lesbian fiction—Mary Daly, Rita Mae. I learned contemporary feminist "things" before I learned "real things." I grew up in women's culture and hardly remember life before it.

And then there was history. I studied it halfheartedly, not really identifying with the world of the past because it was so unlike mine. I used to read the writings of Gertrude Stein or Virginia Woolf and never felt connected. The struggles they were/are having seemed distant and bizarre. It was sort of like "why didn't she play one Chris Williamson album for them? . . . then they'd understand." I was frozen and insulated in my experience and somehow the steps that led up to me never seemed sequential or important.

The closest I have ever come to "getting it" (our man-made language is sorely lacking) is when I saw *The Dinner Party*. The textures and colors were so very wild. . . . I felt with every sense that I was part of a never-beginning, never-ending stream. I knew God/dess and knew that she was only and always on my side.

But what I connected with was not an individual then, it was with a common experience, a common theme of life. The individuals were still "Gertrude Stein and the rest."

Yesterday, I started reading Mary's work. I read it once, again, and even skimmed it a third for the parts I liked. Her story became real to me. I caught a glimpse of what this struggle was for her—caught a glimpse of how we connected with the same pain. Maybe, in male language, it would be as simple as saying that the biography the editors offered at the beginning allowed me to view the writer's life—her ups and downs (depressions)—and therefore I was more able to read the document. Maybe, but that seems barren, and the thing that makes this *all* so exciting is the lack of barrenness . . . whatever the polar opposite of John Calvin could be—I found in Mary Wollstonecraft.

I grieve that she never quite made it into my history books—not particularly the ones we use in grammar and high school because everyone has given up on those. But the ones I used to teach myself. There has got to be a way for the contemporary *un*academic women's community to meet Mary—because I now know that if we/they don't, we/they will wither and die.

I FEEL STRONGER

Eileen Alexa Anderson

In the last few weeks I have probably said "I am a feminist" more than in the preceding thirty-four years of my life. This is significant to me because it is the first time I have chosen to not care whether the claim might be alienating or not. Instead, I view it as a means of clarifying myself to others, a way to stimulate discussion, or possibly as a way of checking overt sexist behavior. I grew up with a "man-hating, bra-burning" concept of feminists. In college I have discovered a general linking of feminism with lesbianism; feminism and the women's movement still meet with generalized fear and stereotyping by both women and men. By identifying myself as a feminist I feel that I can put my face where a blank might have been before and challenge some of those stereotypes without negating the important contributions of each era and group within the women's movement. And each time I say out loud "I am a feminist," I feel stronger in my affiliation.

1. Simone de Beauvoir, *The Second Sex* (New York: Alfred A. Knopf, 1970), 59.

FOUR

Exploring Feminist Perspectives

How might the truth look different?

I read this sentence, and I am arrested by certain words: "look," "different," "How might . . . ?" Truth has a "look": seen from a different angle, truth might wear a different style. With this insight, feminist scholarship generates new knowledge. But perhaps a look is not something truth has or wears, but is also a verb, something "truth" does. With this insight, feminist scholarship moves us to think differently, to develop new frameworks with which to know.

—Ann Burlein

As Ann Burlein's rumination on truth suggests, feminist scholarship causes a change in perspective—what was once taken for granted becomes open to question. True to form, as we wrote this book we found ourselves confronted with a distinction that could not have been made just fifteen years ago: if you are a student, it is one thing to be taking a women's studies course, it is something else altogether to consider yourself a feminist. The readings in the previous section (Engaging Feminism) focus on the ups and downs of emerging as a feminist. The readings in this section explore a variety of issues such as race and class identities, the political nature of knowledge, the impulse toward safe (and separatist) communities, and the difficulties of consciousness raising and common bonds. Yet, all of the contributions begin with a feminist commitment that is a source of strength, reassurance, and new (sometimes troubling) insights.

Both implicitly and explicitly, most of the literature on the theory and practice of women's studies assumes that the practitioners of this new scholarship are feminist faculty who develop courses and design curricula. Yet, as Adrienne Rich reminds her readers in "Taking Women Students Seriously," it is students who should be at the center of the educational process.[1] The lives they lead outside the classroom are rich with data that reinforce or challenge what they are learning in the classroom. Some of the most recalcitrant questions in feminism—How do you at once build community and respect individuality? What are the common grounds and differences between women of color and white women? Should we be focusing on women or gender?—are addressed in the readings that follow. The questions have continued relevance and new meaning for each contributor.

For some undergraduates in women's studies, like Mechelle Evans, Heather Howard, and V. V. Serrant, the idea of a women's culture is intriguing. For other students, exploring feminist perspectives forces them to confront their belief in individualism with their new interest in collective enterprises. Karla Shargent grew up in a family and community where individual effort was seen as the path to every success; her work after college did not dispel that belief. Now, back in the classroom as a graduate student, she sees the subtle and pernicious forms of discrimination that affect her. Similarly, Suzanne Shedd uncovers the patterns of her professional isolation in science only to discover that she has been complicit in perpetuating them. Recognizing that you do not want to be isolated within the academy is a first step toward finding a community of intellectual understanding, personal commitment, peer support. "Feelings of community," says Wendy Wagner of her experiences at a Washington, D.C., rally, make it possible "to use our bodies to speak."

Even so, exploring feminist perspectives also requires developing a voice in order to recognize yourself as an independent, thinking being with both intellectual and personal abilities. Such independence of perspective—trusting your own insights—is a new experience for many women; but developing it is absolutely key to a student's empowerment as an active learner. In its absence, the boundaries between an emotional and an intellectual life can only continue to inhibit the process of self-definition. The writers here record their doubts about themselves, distrusting their ability to sift and winnow information or to see things "as they really are." Silence, powerlessness, and isolation are themes that pervade the writings; these are topics best braved in the safe space of a journal. Community, confi-

57

dence, women friends, and fun also thread through the narratives; the mix makes it possible to be a feminist—and to speak out.

I WANT TO EXPERIENCE WOMEN'S CULTURE

Mechelle R. Evans

Excuse me, Mechelle, who are you?

I am a black woman, an African American. I am a womanist, a feminist, a woman who appreciates her race, gender, class. I have not always been so happy with my womanhood, nor have I always exclaimed it relentlessly. This has occurred gradually over the course of four years. It all came together recently. . . . I had never considered myself a feminist before, but I do now. I want to learn more about the contributions of women in professional fields. I want to experience the women's culture. I enjoy activities where female friends bond through communication, experience, laughter. I do not feel a need to include male counterparts in all activities. This enjoyment did not become conscious though until this semester. I can remember many times cherishing moments with a few female friends and sometimes feeling pressured to invite our male companions later in the evening. This is no longer. I think that as women we should defy the myth of our dependency on men for enjoyment and pleasure. . . .

I have also come to appreciate how we must overcome lines that divide us. We cannot allow classism, intraracism, interracism, politics, or socioeconomics to divide us. We must actively resist and understand that we have common interests, common goals, common bonds. The bottom-line analysis tells us there is a difference between the vagina and the penis. Unfortunately, as an African American I cannot ignore a further reduction of people . . . women, to black and white.

We must keep focused as women and maintain verbal exchange among ourselves. I have learned to appreciate my voice, my choice to follow or refrain, my ability to relish my womanhood.

It is not embarrassing to have menstruation. It is not harmful to explore sexuality. It is not wrong to disregard men sometimes if their voices are uninformed, biased, and irrelevant.

Women have been the strong front for a long time, and I cherish the women in my family who have provided the opportunity for my existence.

A SENSE OF CONTINUITY

Kathryn West

I'm beginning to wonder if I don't want to argue for gender as an (the?) "essential" category. I do not want to ignore men nor do I want to ignore race, class, etc., *but*, it seems to me we've seen a historical pattern that suggests that if you let the conversation shift away from women, they get dropped out of the picture altogether and what's been said time and time again gets forgotten all over again. And, more and more I'm drawn to feeling at a gut level that all women do share some things simply by virtue of being female. *Of course* there are tremendous and important differences that are a function of race, class, sexual orientation, geographic identification—of simply being an individual with experiences different from any one other individual—*yet*, perhaps there are also tremendous and important similarities that come about because of being born female. Maybe those similarities are due to "biology," maybe due to "social conditioning," more likely due to both. . . . I'm particularly interested in the sense of a pattern that's starting to emerge in my own conception of history. It's as if I now have this whole parallel tradition being formulated in my mind of European history from the Middle Ages on (hmmm . . . wonder what was happening with women in the Orient and in Africa and . . .). Now I'm considering the word "parallel," and, yes, I think that is what I want to say. Because although the new sense of history I'm developing has definite and important intersections with the old, traditional version, part of the pattern I'm imagining has to do with this sense of a continued and repeated *separate* women's sphere. It's as if women have had this—not just hidden, silenced history—but a whole world they've created, felt empowered by, and lived in along with *but not in a secondary way* to their participation in the patriarchal world. What I'm trying to say is that I'm not sure yet whether it would be fair to say one world has held primacy for women over the other—I think it would be historically variable on the individual and the collective levels, but that the "other world" we're discovering was at least as important for women as the patriarchal world (again, any primacy of one sphere over the other to women would, I would guess, be a variable matter). And, what's particularly exciting about this is that while at first it seemed to exist as "pockets" of empowered women's spheres popping up at various points in the various places, I'm now starting to feel (and *feel* is the proper word because it suggests both the emotional impact this has for me and my sense of this as at least partially intuitive) a sense of continuity, as if this "other world" has always been there, taking on slightly different forms in different times and different social, economic, and geographical milieus, yet persistent and recognizable as operating from the same— dare I say it?—essence. Well, that was fun!

WE ISOLATE OURSELVES

Heather H. Howard

I think something missing in my education has been a sort of camaraderie with other women. . . . Women need to feel that other women are there for them—at college I haven't even really felt like a woman per se, because I have never really been confronted with a women's issue that personally affected me, so it was easy to remain aloof to the campaigns. Basically, many women feel like they can do anything a man can and that there are no obstacles for them. It's actually very selfish, because we shut out the problem when we are the ones who could do something about it. Although I've been like that, thinking that I could fend for myself and avoid discrimination, I have come to the realization that to a certain extent women *do* need to come together to form *our* agenda. If we do not—that is, if women think they do not need other women because they themselves are not suffering from any gender-based discrimination—then we isolate ourselves.

MY UNDISPUTED DIGNITY

V. V. Serrant

While I have always been aware of the differences between myself and those of a different race or of the other gender, I had never consciously thought about the dynamics behind these complex relationships involving race, gender, and class. The combination of these three issues is used by many in the existing dominant culture to keep women and minorities in a lower level of power. The understanding of my womanhood has opened my mind to a whole new stream of knowledge, thus creating a new awakening of self.

This new self realizes the critical necessity of both the feminist movement and the black women's movement. While ideally the two perhaps should have been working as one, their individuality and the forces powering both have not diminished due to the separation. I am a firm believer in the idea that everything happens for a reason. The need that many black women have felt to form their own organizations has historically resulted in an attack on new issues that had not taken precedence in the feminist movement. With the separation more energy could be directed toward those issues that are uniquely ours rather than weakening and dividing our energies to gear them toward women in general. . . .

It is those black women who fought before me that helped shape my undisputed dignity. While I may not always raise my voice in order to let the world know of my pride, it is always a part of me. When the tides turn and I suffer one of life's pitfalls, it is this "quiet, undisputed dignity of my womanhood" that carries me through.

APPEARING MASCULINE

Charles Paine

Something strange I wrote at the top of my reading notes

At the very beginning of my notes for this reading is this: Sex, sex, sex—sometimes I wish I was more marginalized—but then again, I'm sort of a woman in a man's body and disposition—so I understand.

I honestly don't remember writing these words, which I must have written sometime Saturday, and here it is Wednesday. With the exception of the "Sex, sex, sex," I think I can make out what I was thinking: I was thinking that I feel like such a WASPeM (even though I'm neither Anglo-Saxon nor Protestant); I feel so center-of-the-roadish. Sometimes I envy people who have been marginalized by our society, and the reason for that envy, I think, is because I think if I had experienced more prejudice during my life, perhaps I would be a more independent thinker. I've always been fairly good at assimilating concepts and coming up, occasionally, with new twists on ideas—but I'm sometimes ashamed at my respect for authority, and my fear of change.

And I think it's these habits of thinking and feeling that (1) make me skeptical of new ideas and (2) prevent me from ever becoming an innovative, truly original thinker. That's alright—I've accepted, for the most part, my limitations, but I don't like the way I'm often hesitant about or even scared by new ideas. This fear and hesitancy manifests itself, as it seems to me, in skepticism—maybe more skepticism than is good for me.

I think, for instance, about this other professor I know, a brilliant, friendly, caring, innovative, *confident* young scholar. . . . And I've been to a couple of his lectures, and he works out these complicated and interesting arguments that are based on assumptions that not everybody holds, certainly, but he doesn't let that diminish his assertiveness in the least. Distinguished persons ask him questions about something he hasn't taken into account, and he responds with perfect calmness that certainly that might be taken into account in some other study, but *his* work is not about such things and it would be extraneous.

And I think, I could never do that. I would just assume that there was indeed something wrong with my argument (i.e., with *me*) and because I couldn't account for everything, my argument was therefore weak. And that's what I mean about being "a woman in a man's body and disposition": I act like the typical male, but inside I feel just like typical females in our culture. . . . Whenever I hear about culturally created feminine weaknesses, I always think, "They're talking about me, too." And being a man adds an additional burden: I feel deep down that I'm not *supposed* to act that way, that it's not masculine. And appearing masculine, I think, is something I've got down pretty good. I remember people used to comment on how much self-confidence I had—just blustering on my part or acting out the role, I'd guess. But it takes its toll on the inside, having to act the gender role that is really not me. Now I do *not* mean to imply that I've had it especially hard, harder than women have it—I'm quite aware that being male has afforded me zillions of privileges, without which . . . God, who knows where or what I'd be doing nowadays. But I suppose my point is that I'm very aware of the difficulties of gender stereotyping because the male stereotype is in many ways alien to me, and that causes severe tension inside.

BEING SILENCED

Elana Newman

The whole issue of separatist movements is one I struggle with both ideologically and personally. While I think there are firm theoretical grounds for such actions, I find it difficult to accept socially and politically. When I became most interested in feminist thought while studying at a very leftist school in Britain, I was ostracized from the women's group for a number of reasons including my religion, nationality, and sexual orientation. In one of the most traumatic intellectual periods of my life, I attended a meeting in which we were to address the schism in the feminist movement between lesbians and heterosexuals. Twenty lesbians appeared at that meeting, two people including myself who defined themselves as heterosexual, and one woman who defined herself as asexual. For three hours I struggled with addressing our commonalities but instead was basically harassed, affronted, and oppressed. It was personally a very difficult time for me, because I felt like in trying to expand our views and communicate, we repeated and reenacted the social structure. It was the first time I personally experienced being silenced; while I think I learned a lot from that period, it also made me struggle with that issue and its ramifications, so I am sensitive to considering those issues and figuring out my position. At present I think all intellectual, social movements require individuals with varying degrees of "radicalism" in order to be effective in facilitating change in the culture, but I worry about the ultimate good of not being able to have channels of productive dialogue.

THE POWERLESSNESS OF INDIVIDUALISM

Karla G. Shargent

I picked up the message that "it was time women stopped complaining about lack of opportunity" not only in college but also way back in high school. I had done well enough in high school to take my pick of the colleges which interested me. I chose the one considered the toughest. St. Olaf has close ties to the Lutheran church; as students we were often told how privileged we were and that we should feel a responsibility after college to "give back" some of what had been so graciously given to us. There were no distinctions based on gender in this message. Countless examples were paraded before us of both women and men alumni who had gone on to be doctors, teachers, pastors, lawyers, musicians, missionaries, and Peace Corps volunteers. The focus was on what we as individuals could, and should, do with the many gifts and talents which we had been able to develop while at school. If and when we did get married, it was hoped that it was to someone who felt the same way as we did about serving others, so that it would be agreeable to both partners to continue this work while raising a family.

Am I making myself clear? I was mostly taught to consider myself as an isolated, individual human being who could go as far as my own personal talents, skills, and ambitions would take me. My perception of myself as part of a community or group is very limited. It was never hammered into me very forcefully that limitations might be placed on me just because I happened to be a member of a certain group. I did not realize that my being a woman, an American, a small-town Midwesterner, a member of the middle class, etc., might determine very profoundly how others would perceive me and, especially, how it might place serious limitations on how far my talents and ambitions could otherwise carry me.

After college I spent a few years out in the business world. I *did* encounter there several instances where people responded to me as if I were *only* a woman or a Midwesterner. That is, they saw me only through the prism of whatever group or community they had assigned me to, and did not view me as someone with very special, individual skills. It bothered me but was really no more than a minor hassle. I shrugged it off. I felt they were too stupid to know better—that it was more their loss than mine. Besides, I knew I wasn't going to be there forever; I was going back to school.

Of course, everyone told me that school would present its own special problems. But I thought I would be able to handle them better, especially since this was where I really wanted to be. Well, the reality has turned out to be a bit more complex than that. The prejudices I have encountered at Duke are much less blatant than in the company I worked for, and for just that reason much more dangerous. I'm also beginning to realize here at Duke that our circumstances are much more determined by our "membership" in certain groups than I had ever been led to believe.

What I'm really trying to say is that I'm just beginning to realize how powerless I am as an individual. My powerlessness is all the more poignant since I'm a member of a class of people—women—who have been, and are, oppressed by society as a whole. I need feminism?!?

ALIENATION

Stacey W.

I left Durham/Duke this weekend. Friday afternoon came around, and I felt I couldn't deal with this place, with being alone here, with an empty apartment, with work and lack of motivation and nothing really fun to look forward to. I knew that if I stayed I would get *really* depressed—more so than I was when I left, more so than I felt I was, anyway, being home. But leaving didn't solve anything—it just helped me momentarily cope, or push away what I couldn't cope with. Loneliness, "alienation"—Tonight I came back and this friend made me deal with it—with my leaving, my "problem solving," my action (and before I continue, I want to clarify that although I don't think this fact of my "leaving" is in and of itself such a monumental crux in my life, it does provide a place on which I can focus my thoughts here). The most ironic aspect of all this is that in the paper I just wrote on Toni Morrison's *Sula*, I talked about precisely this problem of leaving, and how our culture—American/postmodern—often constructs leaving as the only option, positing individual survival at the expense of any more fundamental, communal understanding and change. In my paper, I tied this option to the construction of masculinity in Morrison's world, and how the solutions that construction enables actually function to preserve the systems of domination and forms of internalized oppression that determine it in the first place intact. Having dealt with these problems, questions, options "in theory," here I was, nevertheless, choosing the same option for myself because I didn't know how, or couldn't, or was too scared to actually reach out and say to someone: "I need you. Be there for me. Help me/us work through what makes this place, our shared context, situation so unbearable, so difficult to handle, so unlivable." Saying this would have meant putting myself on the line, and I was feeling too vulnerable and alone to do that. So I left, and nothing has changed (except maybe inside me)—the potential for the same thing to happen again, for the same feelings to recur, remains.

Only I came back, and I talked about it to someone who understands because she's been feeling it—isolation, disconnection, loneliness, lack of emotional support—too. And maybe our talking will make a difference—maybe next time, or the time after that, when I'm feeling alone or isolated or depressed, I won't just run away, go home to mommy. Maybe I will try to deal with this place, and build the friendships, the connections, the networks of people who care and who feel as strongly as I do about changing this graduate school, university setting—about breaking through the patterns of interaction, the systems of thought/learning that inhibit communication, sharing, bonding between students and instead encourage isolated competition, isolated success stories, isolated production, and excellence above and beyond the "masses," the group. Sisterhood is powerful. This question of leaving for me ties in so deeply to the issue of control with which I began this reflection. I felt I was in control when I left, when I went home, and to a certain extent I was—I was choosing to change my situation in order to "survive"/cope. But I was also choosing to do so by confirming my belief in self-reliance, in individual action, in the notion that I alone am responsible first and foremost for myself—and for no one else. I, as individual, as Stacey, took off, was capable of doing so; my decision seems in some ways equivalent to that of the anorexic who decides to prove how much she is in control by refusing to eat, to be dependent on food, to pay attention to her needs, her hunger. And both prove futile/ineffective escapes. After all, I carried all my pain with me. The knots this place tied inside me remained.

Returning, I realized that I also left this friend who may have needed me this weekend when I was gone. I broke a trust by leaving, a connection to an individual whom I desperately need, and who also would have made me face that from which I was running—she would have asked why I was doing this, she would have made me face these needs that weren't being filled. And she could have, to some extent, filled them. Only I didn't (couldn't?) give her a chance then. I could do so only when I returned. Tonight. And she was angry with me for leaving. Because I had not just acted for myself—my actions had repercussions for us both. I may be "free," but only relatively so, and there is so much joy in learning that my freedom is only relative, and that there is connection with different people here that gives my notion of self-reliance, self-control the lie.

Our talk tonight seems to share a lot of that which I find most valuable in consciousness-raising groups—it hints at their necessity for overcoming internalized oppression, as well as in overcoming the dominant structures that determine that oppression, identifying them to shatter their effects. How do we begin to fight the "feminization" of poverty in this country, how do we begin to speak to one another about the forces that determine the global economic disadvantage of women? I think this type of discussion begins or at least proceeds through such consciousness-raising efforts that allow self-recovery beyond/outside the classroom. Which brings me to my next point—my talk with this friend tonight highlighted the need for this kind of communication/discussion to happen not only within the classroom setting, not only within women's studies courses or the university, but in our "unprofessional" lives as well. It's too easy to construct the barriers between personal and political needs by intellectualizing some to the extent that they become only academic or political—that is, detached (neutral, objective, disembodied, unfelt). It still amazes me that I can write about an issue like "leaving," running away from one's problems, forsaking social responsibilities, that I can deal with this issue intellectually and still not see myself functioning the same way, reacting emotionally to something in a way I understand "rationally" to be self-defeating. It's at points like these that I see what the phrase "making the personal political" means for me—daring to question personal motivations for action or lack thereof behind all our (implicitly, if not explicitly, political) actions (like leaving, writing). But it is also at such points that I begin to wonder what the relation between my theory of action (that is, confronting through mutual understanding and sharing those situations, laws, circumstances that disrupt our peace) and my own emotional needs is—where these two short circuit. While I understand, while I believe that only by confronting those things that threaten to destroy me/us shall I/we be able to overcome them, I am aware that this means asking a great deal of myself/people who perhaps are not psychically prepared to "perform" accordingly. While in theory, the best avenue for me in retrospect seems to have been to stay put and deal with what being here might mean, I was incapable of doing so. Why? Is it because I have been trained (in ideology) to deal with unpleasure in my life in a particular way (by running away from it), or is it because my self-defense mechanisms are so well tuned that I can sense when something will be too much and I do what I have to do to get by? I am uncomfortable taking either position, or even only both—so much seems to be involved in how and why people respond to victimization and oppression and simple unhappiness in particular ways.

What keeps coming back to me, though, is the need for dialogue beyond the immediate coping response. Coping is good and necessary—but it's not enough. I think to myself—OK, I left, but I came back, and I talked about it with someone who cares and who would understand. And together we reached new answers, new coping strategies. And perhaps my leaving facilitated that for us both. And there is a value in this aspect of my action, in the consciousness raising that followed therefrom. But this conversation would not have happened had I not come back—the emphasis, therefore, must be placed on the return, the dialogue, the sisterhood, not on the immediate coping strategy.

THE IDEA THAT YOU'RE "SPECIAL"

Suzanne Franks Shedd

I had convinced myself, or had been convinced, that I was special because of what I was doing, and that other women who *weren't* striving to be engineers or "hard" scientists were just wimps who weren't trying and weren't as good as me. (Part of this is the "exceptional woman" syndrome, part is the general prejudice of "science" against the "liberal arts.") But you spend time trying to neutralize your ability, to soothe the egos of male classmates; yet you know that you are still excluded and so you tend this secret little anger inside of yourself. And . . . because there are more women in, for example, engineering than there were twenty-five years ago, your status as "exceptional" is distorted. Yes, it's normal for women to do this, we encourage them to (or at least don't discourage them), but, no, we're not going to treat you "just like the boys." You're not equal—your classmates resent you, female friends find you a mystery, males in social situations are intimidated by you. So you get lonely, and then you take comfort in the idea that you're "special." Society creates a category, you move into it; then you have certain experiences that end up making you reinforce and perpetuate the category. You really begin to believe you're different and superior, at the same time that you feel different and inferior. This effectively blocks you from uniting with other women, having any sense of solidarity, and from doing anything to change society.

[Later in the semester:] I now can see myself in a chain of women stretching backwards and forwards in time. The strength of knowing your history is that a large part of the space you need gets created (in your mind). Then you feel better armed to go out and create it in the world.

THE RALLY

Wendy Wagner

Yesterday I marched in the largest rally ever held in Washington, D.C. I marched with both women and men, shouted with women and men, cheered with women and men, felt triumph with women and men—solely for the rights of women.

Despite the wonderful amount of support by men and the absence of overt sexism in the march, what I remember most are the feelings of community with women and the awe we all felt as we approached the Washington Monument, awe at the incredible numbers of people. We saw about two hundred people from Duke, mostly undergraduate women (a nice surprise). Three hundred thousand people total, and it felt like more. It felt like the whole world. And when we finally got to the Capitol—it was a struggle to decide between savoring every step of the march and reading every sign and smiling at every person and wanting to get to the Capitol and sit(!) and listen to the speakers—and when we finally got to the Capitol it was the most beautiful sight. I wanted to capture it on film, but I couldn't. You see, what was so central to the picture I wanted to capture was the *movement*. I think I now know why we use the word "movement" to describe political activity; it was certainly a prochoice movement.

When we got to the Capitol to hear the speakers, it was like the triumph we felt had replaced the blood in our veins. Do you know that feeling when you're light-headed from exhaustion and the only thing that keeps you going is happiness? We were exhausted, excited, and proud—but mostly triumphant because we'd never seen so goddam many people in our lives, much less making a political statement like the one we were making.

I've come to realize that the central issue of women's rights is not whether women are rational, thinking human beings; the problem with the earlier feminists (Wollstonecraft, etc.) is that they thought that once women's minds were free their bodies would be free also. This is not the case—women can and have always been free to think what they like. They are just not permitted to act on their thoughts—and acting means speaking, breathing, yelling, teaching, marching, walking, running—anything that involves bodily activity. We speak, they muzzle us; we breathe, they put us in corsets and/or tight jeans; we yell, we get put in sanatoriums; we teach, we get the worst rooms; we march, walk, run, they put us in long skirts and high heels. It's all been a question of what we do with and where we place our bodies. We can think all the radical thoughts we want to, but if we dare to use our bodies to speak, if we dare to put our bodies in a public forum, then we must be stopped.

That was what was so wonderful about yesterday. We all made choices about our bodies: we placed them in Washington and we did it in concert. And we damn near filled that whole city—*physically, materially*. That was the real triumph.

MIDWIVES TO EACH OTHER

Judith W. Dorminey

I came to Durham a day early this week so I could meet with Naomi and Vanessa to plan tomorrow's class and so I would be here to hear Toni McNaron speak about discovering the self in academia or some such thing. Now those two things have happened and I am luxuriating in the solitude and silence of a single room at the hotel. Tomorrow I will bum around Perkins Library and the used book store until time for class and then head back to my everyday reality. In the meantime I will write about this very pleasant and amazing day.

Vanessa and Naomi met me at the Ninth Street Bakery. I lunched on a cheese croissant and a cup of black currant tea—the drive from Charlotte always makes me very hungry (so what doesn't?). We began discussing the reading material and immediately discovered that we were miles apart on every article. At times the conversation got heated, although nobody ever called anybody else "Meathead." When we had wrangled away most of the afternoon, we called it quits and agreed to meet just before class to finalize our plan for the seminar.

I don't know when I've enjoyed an afternoon more. Naomi and Vanessa are my two favorite class members anyway—I can't imagine how we were put together as facilitators, but it pleased me immensely—and to match wits with them at leisure was one of the most delightful things that's happened to me in graduate school. One of the very sad parts of being "just a housewife" is the limited conversation available to you even if you do manage to break out of the isolation. The Naomis and Vanessas have preserved my sanity for the last few years. Anyway the afternoon was wonderful, and I will treasure the memory of such good company.

And just when I thought my cup runneth over, Toni McNaron showed up in East Duke Building, and I'll never be the same. It was astounding to me to meet a woman with whom I had so much and so little in common. I am Hattie Heterosexual Housewife—she is Toni Terrific Teacher and Scholar. Yet we speak with the same accents (she says "line" for *lion*— I say "al" for *owl*); we suffer the same oppressions in different arenas; we talk with words and communicate with metaphors; we are both surprised at the energy and the power and the fresh beginning that comes for a middle-aged woman, and no one told either one of us about it ahead of time. So she is doing her seeking in public, and I am doing mine in private, and we are both filled with wonder.

I probably would have liked her anyway just because she was an interesting and spunky person, but as she talked her genuine kindness and love for people glowed through. As she spoke of her students and how she dealt with them, I was reminded of women trading mother wisdom over neighborhood coffee.

Most of all I was interested in her search for a new relationship to younger women. As she said, she was old enough now to be their biological mother, but she was not their mother. She also seemed to be aware of how much she could learn and gain from them as well as what she had to offer. It seems to me that there is a new way for women to be with each other across the generations that hasn't existed before. I can't put my finger on it and apparently neither can McNaron, but somehow I seem to be part of a generation that has never existed before: no longer at-home, nose-wiping mothers—not yet and maybe never-to-be cookie-baking grandmothers—biological obligations met, bodies still strong, minds still lucid, and spirits open to new possibilities. Perhaps we are the first cohort with a chance to escape gender and to see how life might be lived if one could be gender free. Toni is beginning to explore the concept from her perspective, I am doing the same. There must be lots of us. It's a good time to be forty-seven and a woman.

And so to bed.

Dream (True and in Technicolor)

I am in the beautiful reception room in East Duke Building—the same room where Toni spoke earlier and where my class will meet in the afternoon. Now the room is empty except for two me's. One is the me who watches the me who does things. The watching me is the same woman who stood at the foot of the delivery table and saw my children being born; she is the woman who knows who is calling before the phone rings; she conjures up people and books and sometimes other objects when the doing me needs them; she's a strange one but not to be denied.

I (the doing me, the one people call Judy) am in the center of the blue and rust and white medallion woven into the middle of the great blue rug that covers the wood floor. The medallion's borders contain a bird that could be an eagle or a phoenix and some flowers that defy identification. I am surrounded by a circle of empty antique chairs. Overhead the chandelier blazes with the light of cream-colored candles. I am half-squatting, arms and legs akimbo, looking for all the world like a statue of an early fertility goddess.

As the watching me attends, I strain and groan and grunt and hold my swollen belly. I struggle and struggle all alone except for the silent watching me. I see my face turn red, watch my eyes scrunch shut, and see me push and push and push until in a great gush of sound and water and blood and joy I give birth to a messy, kicking, yelling baby. I know and the watching me knows that the baby is also me. Before either of us can hold her or clean her up, she steps over to the bird woven into the carpet medallion. As she stands there, she grows into a shadowy woman whose face cannot be seen clearly. She is holding a glass partially filled with water. She does not yet have a name.

I wake in the dark of the room of the hotel and turn on the bedside light. Plenty of time to read and enjoy the dream and the day. It's a long time until dawn—

Thoughts on the Class

The discussion went well enough I think. Vanessa, Naomi, and I never did settle our differences but we managed to facilitate despite that. I guess we are shining examples of feminist collaboration in which difference is incorporated into reality because it *is* reality instead of having to be eliminated in order to give a monolithic (phallic) structure to reality. At any rate most people participated in the talk. As we had hoped, each of them addressed the metaquestions and the specific questions as applied to their respective disciplines. That informed the rest of us and probably stimulated some thought in the commentator herself.

After my dream last night, I saw the parlor with different eyes. Now it seems to me to be a huge womb—a private, safe place where we are all giving birth to ourselves and to each other and to a new way of looking at the world. The stern men in the pictures on the wall can only watch with no power to interfere or influence what is happening before their eyes. Their presence reminds us of the world we will have to deal with when the lovely, fanlighted double doors open for us, but for now the men are on the periphery of our room and our business. For now we are midwives to each other and don't need them.

It seems significant to me that this group has never evolved a seating plan. Usually in a classroom situation even when there are not any assigned seats people begin to take the same seat each time. In my women's studies seminar the seating changes each week. The closest thing to regular seat choices seems to be the three subgroups of sofa-sitters—those who always choose the sofas, those who sometimes do, and the never-sit-that-close-to-someone-else people. Otherwise we are always turning and shifting and facing different people for our conversations. Reminds me of three little Dormineys who were always turning and shifting when they were getting ready to come change my world. They did not always make me comfortable, but at least I knew they were alive.

1. Adrienne Rich, *On Lies, Secrets, and Silence* (New York: Norton, 1979), 237–45, esp. 244–45.

FIVE

Reassessing Classrooms

Sooner or later, women's studies students realize that they are seeking an education within an environment that is predicated on the exclusion of women. It is not only that some (or many) individual faculty members resist learning about the new scholarship on women. It is not only that the generic "he" in textbooks ignores women. It is not only that the culture of some disciplines seems especially unwelcoming to women. It is not only that women students rarely have women teachers. It is not only that the competitive standards of classroom performance make many women ill at ease. It is all of these—as the following readings suggest.

Moreover, though there are words of praise for some women's studies classes in these pages, the contributors' critiques of their classroom experiences focus on structures of authority that can exist inside or outside of the women's studies classroom. Just as there is no accepted orthodoxy on the use of journals, there is no accepted orthodoxy on the use of traditional authority structures in women's studies classrooms. In the absence of a sustained critical literature, individual pedagogical experiments are episodic—abandoned if they do not work, recommended to colleagues if they do, but reinvented by others elsewhere as the need arises—and this, too, is the case both inside and outside of the women's studies classroom. The students, then, must adjust to the individual styles of their teachers. All too often, due to the sheer weight of the Academic Tradition, those teaching styles assume too little about the students' abilities and too much about the teachers'.

In the planning stages, we had trouble articulating our sense of the glue that stuck the extracts in this section together. At first we called it the "Tensions" section because the contributors speak to the tensions between the particularities of a discipline—its vocabulary, its standards of excellence, its philosophical grounding—and the nature of the interdisciplinary research women's studies requires.

Next we decided that tension did not accurately describe the quality of the critique that all of these contributions share; so we retitled it "What is a nice girl like me doing in a place like this?" The second title did a better job of representing the tensions as personal encounters with institutionalized practices of exclusion. The students' critique of gender as a social system had moved from a reconsideration of those experiences remembered (including families, friends, and first encounters with feminist ideas) to the experiences of the present, everyday life. And for these contributors, much of that everyday life takes place within the classroom environment, within the student-teacher relationship, and within growing, disquieting realizations.

The students are not allowed to speak about their disquieting thoughts outside the privacy of their journals, because their thoughts are nothing less than heretical. Denouncing the grind of faculty demands on graduate students, they speak to the ways that the academic environment is modeled on the worst of the norms for white, Western male, father/son relations—competitive, unsupportive, sometimes hostile battling to confront and outperform one another. This is an environment protected and privileged as the system by which the best and the brightest will shine. Those who do not "shine" thus fail from their own inadequacies. They are disempowered, silenced, and left to blame only themselves. Women choose not to become scientists and mathematicians, or they drop out of graduate school, or they set aside their passion for one topic in order to do the paper, the research, that professors and their departmental agendas recognize as "valid."

Alice Nelson, facing prelims, finds that she has internalized the arcane language of the academy and she explores how this affects her ability to teach "other-wise." Undergraduate Mara Amster wonders about the place of "maybe" in a scientific worldview that seems to leave no room for doubt. Amy C. confronts familiar questions in feminist challenges to the traditional curriculum—questions with personal relevance: Who creates standards of excellence? How do these standards apply to me as I try to bring new material and new approaches into my research?

So, from the margins of the classroom, these voices speak out against the petty coercions and the grand exclusions; and sometimes, as the final contribution suggests, they find a way to make themselves heard.

WOMEN ALREADY THINK

Ginger Brent

If feminists merely aim to grant women access to traditional ways of proving that they are intelligent, they may obscure the fact that women already think, and that their forms of knowledge have enabled them to contribute to society and are therefore valuable. Furthermore, if women aim to "master" the texts celebrated by the academy, what they may be absorbing are a series of arguments validating the ideology that labels them inferior. . . . Since I know that whenever I'm disturbed about something and try to think of ways to alter the situation, I am likely to overlook the real cause of a problem because I'm obsessed with the symptom, I have been grateful for the constant reminder that sometimes both the way we define dilemmas and the way we conceive of solutions reflects the very system that's created the tension, and that we must vigorously examine our premises if we want genuine change.

RACISM GOES UNDERGROUND

Deborah K. Chappel

During the semester I taught my first writing course, I assigned "Letter from Birmingham Jail." I had two black students in my classroom—both scholarship athletes—and it was the week students were marching for Martin Luther King's birthday. We discussed the structure and literary features of the essay, we discussed nonviolent protest and debated it a little, but I didn't feel good about the class. Something was missing. I was never sure exactly what that was.

When I student-taught several years ago, I had to teach *To Kill a Mockingbird* to juniors in high school—each class had between twenty-eight and thirty white students and between one and four black students. I felt like with all our good-sounding talk about how bad racism was, we were somehow embarrassing the few black students in the class, taking away their right to anger, speaking for them. Harper Lee's novel was considered progressive in her day; in 1986, its message seemed outdated. In the end, I felt like I was saying, "See? Not all black men are rapists."

Then last spring I taught a course on modern southern literature. Naturally, race was an issue in practically everything we read. Again, we had three black students, two of whom were on the football team, and I always sounded a little more angry about racism than any of them did, a little more anxious to discuss a topic they would just as soon not mention. And this made me angry, the way I'm occasionally and wrong-headedly angry and impatient at my female students who resist feminism.

What this makes me think about is how the whole humanistic approach to race and gender, which is what I guess I've been adopting all along, is basically very flawed. . . . It's the idea, I guess, that racism is a social ill which can be cured with knowledge. Now, class, I'm going to give you the truth about black people and you can stop oppressing them. Got that? The way teachers at all levels assume a kind of "enlightenment" that allows us to light a candle for someone else in darkness. Knowledge isn't enough. It only creates this facade so that the racism goes underground, becomes submerged and more subtle. I've always thought that civil rights made wonderful gains, and some gains have been made, I suppose. I saw the adoption of Martin Luther King into the civil religion of America as a positive thing; it's damned un-American to speak against Martin Luther King these days. I think that's a good thing, really. It's also dangerous. You can't call me prejudiced when I include "Letter from Birmingham Jail" in my syllabus, can you? I'm harder to fight. I take the wind from the black student's sails, the surliness from his (or her) glance. I give him knowledge that's not about him at all, really, and I help to foreclose the possibility of social change. That's what is so disturbing behind the whole presentation of knowledge as a tool to eradicate prejudice or any social ill, including sexism—increased awareness without social activism for change doesn't help at all.

I don't feel so uncomfortable presenting articles on gender or making arguments about gender. I'm not sure why. I think I'm always aware on this issue that telling people about the problem won't cure it; the problem's real for me, and exists on a very complex level. When I read about black women, I don't know what to think or say. It seems appropriate to say how oppressed they are, how awful it is, etc. But I feel I'm ventriloquizing.

I BECOME INVISIBLE

Ann Burlein

There are spaces in which I become invisible, moments when my feet grow leaden, my body stiff. When I shrink so small that my muscles no longer remember how to move, I do the only thing I then know: as an antidote to invisibility, I practice attending to the silences, empty spaces, rejections, and refusals that tumble me over the edge and down the rabbit hole that has no bottom. I watch what happens when I am made to fade: how I direct my eyes down and in, held fast by the double blade of contradictory desire: summoning all my strength so that I am not seen while wanting nothing so much as to be seen for me.

Becoming invisible doesn't take much—just some catalyst stepping in every now and then to kick the appropriate mechanisms: Newton's god. I do the rest, like clockwork. Fears fasten eagle wings to my feet and I flee, so sure that the world can render my desires impossible that I hail the future as already past—the perfect prophet. . . . I run myself into the ground running their race to its completion, tricked once again out of acquiring the tools I need; tricked once again into upholding the status quo. . . .

After three years of graduate school, I find myself undoing, carefully, strand by strand, an invisibility imposed as a condition of entry, unwritten stipulation in a contract I signed without knowing. To walk this campus is constantly to "pass." I see nothing of myself here. I bear no mark: my working-class immigrant parents, my sexualities, even my femaleness go unseen. Unseen by others, I cease to see myself. . . . Claiming an education, I claim my presence.

Yet the identification between claiming an education and claiming my presence confuses. As I fight to do academic feminist work I find myself escalating the "importance" of what I do, until I no longer recognize myself in the portrait I paint. Can't I do this work and be me? . . . I sit in this group and watch myself withdraw. My inside grows large, devours my field of vision and sense of self until I . . . fall into these self-depths. The surface of my body does not represent me here; I feel no home but this "in"side, a material reality which I "know" does not exist but which nevertheless (or therefore) becomes my only truth, the sum total of what I am and can be. . . . This room constantly requires me to forsake my world for another context in which I am no place and no one. So I check at the door the parts of myself I value most. Why speak, when I know before opening my mouth that alien words from an inadmissible context will make the other students uncomfortable. . . . I can speak as they do; I can speak as their other; but I do not know how to speak from a center position. . . .

At home I cry, struggle one more time with my silence. I've fought this battle for years. Now, at a time in my life when I no longer doubt the worth of what I have to say, when I feel certain that I have good things to say which will not be said if I do not say them, still I cannot speak. I hate this silent/silenced part of me. I would excise her if I could, if I knew how.

PRELIM BLUES

Alice Nelson

Prelim Blues,
    Doesn't have a tune, only an echooooooooooo.

Pressure. To "perform." Hoops   I jump through
    read read read leer leer leer male writers escritoires
male academic questions answer answer answer don't worry about
    this, that is much more important don't worry about *that*,
this is much more important, I'll see what I can

        do.
        Can do.
    Yes, it is remarkable that on my list spanning roughly ten centuries of Spanish and four centuries of Spanish American lit. three women "broke into the ranks"—*Never stand in front of a loaded canon.* Unless you have to. And you have to to unload it. Unless you're sporting the latest in bullet-proof attire, or a bullet-proof
        voice.
        Be your own kinda reader, yes, that I will.

    Prioritizing (albeit temporarily) in a way that's not the way that
    I would prioritize and try like hell to do it
        all.
    For whom? For me. I think. As long as I can hold on to I can hold

on.   Remember: dead
                    lines can be liberating.

THE QUEST TO BE OTHER-WISE

Alice Nelson

I've learned something about jargon. I thought I had really shied away
from overusing literary pet words. But I've been startled and horrified of
late to find that I've internalized some concepts in jargon, and that the
words (jargon) I use to express them no longer strike me as jargon, but
rather as the clearest way to express what I'm thinking about in order to be
understood. But such is not the case in broader audiences, the very audiences with whom I wished to communicate when I entered this institution
in the first place. Conformity with it, though, was not supposed to happen. I wonder at the great assimilating power of Discipline, Academia,
which I both aspire to and resist. (Paradox again?) And how the doctoral
examination process (or my dealing with it) has diminished my resistance
and groomed my conformity. I'm finding my exams taxing on many levels.
Whew—constant reassessment is the key.

Another preoccupation: The quest to teach other-wise.

LANGUAGE IS A FASCINATING THING

Claire O'Barr

Language is a fascinating thing. I can remember arguing with my mother
and saying "*Mom*, it doesn't matter whether you use 'he' or 'he or she'—
everyone knows what you mean!" But, of course, later I realized that it
does matter—it matters a lot. I've come to the point now that when I read
things I find sexist, I am not only irritated, but I sincerely feel left out—
as if I'm purposefully not supposed to be included. . . .

I was in my adviser's office and we were talking about a paper I'd written
for her that I wasn't very happy with. She was telling me all the good things
about it and said that I was (am) a good writer. I started laughing. Of all
the positive things I could say about myself, being a good writer isn't one
and I don't get told that very often. She asked why I don't think I'm a good
writer, and I told her it was because I used simple sentence structure and

basic words. She goes, "Oh, not that again!" and proceeded to talk about patriarchal elitist language and said she thought that the most profound statements are even stronger when placed in clear language. I've thought a lot about this, and I agree with her.

PERFORMING IN CLASS

Mary R. Bowman

There are a few things on my mind as I reflect on how I find myself feeling in class. I feel always under scrutiny, as if there is a danger of, and danger in, saying something "wrong" or even something not useful. That kicks in especially when I feel uncertain of my facts or the context or when I'm just starting to explore an idea. But then when I feel confident and have some knowledge to contribute, I feel all the more vulnerable, because then I have less excuse for saying something stupid, and I also feel like I'm also showing off or talking down to people somehow. . . .

For me, speaking in class is always *performing*. I realized this when it struck me that my journal writing feels that way too. I think there is a degree to which this is inevitable—it's not really possible to escape entirely the feeling of being on display to be evaluated, and the concomitant desire to "get it right"—but I think it can be lessened, and I want to try to keep that in mind as a goal. . . .

I think that being in a women's studies seminar has made me a little more attentive to the ways in which I interact with other people in class. There seems to me to be less of an atmosphere in which class discussion is a vehicle for impressing the professor and less of a sense of competitiveness—not so much an effort to outshine others so much as simply to prevent being outshone by them. I'm not sure how much of that is due to the overall dynamics of the class, the attitudes and behaviors of other people, and how much is due to my own increased attention to the question in a course where that kind of thing seems more relevant to the declared subject matter of the course. I do think that both elements are operative. And certainly that aspect of the seminar is going to make me more conscious of those kinds of issues in the future, and I think that's important. Not only in the classroom, but also in other arenas. I think the show-off style that regrettably some classes fall into and some professors tend to foster also occurs in published work and in delivered papers—there often seems to be more interest in being pizzazzy than in really caring about and being engaged with the work. And to me that's regrettable.

I do think that my facility in contributing to class discussions has improved over the course of the semester, although there is still room for improvement yet. That's been partly helped, I think, by the feedback that I've gotten (and also my increasing ability to appreciate the feedback, due in part to my unlearning the show-off model of talking). One of the problems I have is that I often have ideas that I'm not sure how to articulate, and the fear is always present of speaking and being totally uncommunicative. And I've gotten responses to some of my attempts that have shown me that indeed I got at least some part of my meaning across. And that, I think, has improved my confidence.

A MODEL OF INTELLECTUAL EXCHANGE

Angela Hubler

The reading group—it's really important to me. I don't think I would be very happy here in terms of my own work if it wasn't here. I guess I feel kind of trapped in my department. I want to do more than just read stories about women—I don't feel that is adequate. In order to read stories about women you have to understand the entire context of women's lives. I guess the reading group is an ongoing attempt to do that.

In terms of the way in which you *learn*, the group is a lifesaver to me as well. I get so tired of "classroom behavior." Both students and professors are very performance oriented—people want to look smart. It is all so *pretentious*—in terms of the vocabulary, style, etc. It makes me want to puke—especially since within this setting, everyone gets sort of carried away. Even the least pretentious person either becomes unbearable—or is completely silenced, one coping mechanism. . . .

I guess this is sometimes a problem in our group because we've been disagreeing, though we seemed to do so pretty well last time. Maybe this is just a problem for me—conflict and confrontation make my heart pound pound pound.

So, what I want from this group is the safe, nurturant space which is so lacking in every other part of my life. I want that safe home where I can have useful productive discussions about what is so important for me. This space, this model of intellectual exchange is a *goal* for me—something I want to reproduce in the classes which I teach. I think it is a real alternative.

I know that when the group is coming up I start feeling a sense of relief, that soon I can relax, that rejuvenation is on the way, I can soon let my defenses down.

IT AIN'T "PURELY ACADEMIC"

Lisa T.

Deferential language . . . though I did tell my department chair to fuck off the other day, during my oral exam, no less. OK, not in those exact words, but he got the message. And I said fuck off, interestingly enough, when he said, "If you think the elitism and oftentimes sexism of the baroque aesthetic limits its 'potential subversion,' in your words, then why are you here? I mean, why not just take your placard and go out and march somewhere else?" Hit me with your best shot, Mr. Chair, but my you did strike a nerve. A question of this theory/praxis dichotomy which I really think/ hope is false, but then again, couldn't it just be a glorified justification of our raison d'être? While I believe in the power of language to make a difference, for example, the unwritten codes of Academia impose, for "success" (survival even), an increasingly esoteric vocabulary, an increasingly narrow audience. To be able to *not* do that, you've gotta do it well for a while. In the meantime, I march there and argue here. But undoubtedly, insights from my classes and work feed directly into my activism, and vice versa— and it ain't "purely academic." But the overwhelming pressure, the semi-isolation of academic work (I felt especially while preparing for prelims) do seem to push toward a certain "hypocrisy" of "preaching" more than "practicing," though again, I feel much better about things when I assert that these two categories can be mutually inclusive.

I stick at it with faith—a great deal of faith in teaching/education as dissemination and potential change—at the same time that I don't wish to grow complacent: I wonder, doubt, feel guilty for the elitist trappings of the trade.

SCIENCE AND I AREN'T INTIMATES

Connie E. Pearcy

Week One

Although science and I aren't intimates at this stage in my life, we have had a long and relatively pleasant relationship. I took science classes throughout high school and seriously contemplated going into medicine my junior year. I loved biology and tolerated chemistry (I had no self-confidence when it came to experiments; I never believed in the accuracy of my results). I ranked among the best in all the science and math courses I took (granted my high school class was only 150, but it was competitive to the point of absurdity). My science teachers challenged and encouraged me. And to this day, a biology class that tired, frustrated, and enthralled me to no end remains one of my most memorable positive education experiences.

After detailing my long-standing interest in science, I once again question what happened. Having taken two science courses in college, I have yet to complete my science/math graduation requirement. I abandoned plans for medical school as I entered college, and the only reason I offered myself for my decision was I didn't want to spend years studying (I am now considering attending graduate school in history). For some reason, I envisioned medicine or high school teaching as my only options in science. Medicine was too imposing and teaching too limiting for me to go the science route.

I don't really know what all this means. My cop-out rationale may or may not have any broader significance. Everyone must make decisions about which of their interests to pursue. But why I made my decision to steer clear of science and math when all the odds favored those fields is an interesting question to pose.

Week Four

In thinking more about me and math/science, I've come to the tentative conclusion that (1) I would have probably done well in college math courses, (2) no one encouraged me to see the long-term possibilities for me as a mathematician—I still have little grasp of the practical uses for a math major—(3) therefore, I turned my interest to other areas. These other areas may be as uncertain/foreign to me as math, but they were not billed as extremely difficult. They also seemed less confining. I was not required to make a decision about my life course to major in history, but I felt I needed to be extremely committed to a certain career to major in math.

Rather than assume all mathematically gifted people end up in math courses or focus their intellectual energies developing their math skills (in and out of the classroom), I think we need to question the way bright girls are tracked into different fields.

MAYBE

Mara Ilyse Amster

Ever since I was a young child, I have loved the concept of "maybe." The idea of not having a single answer to any given question but rather having the ability to pose an infinite number of theories or hypotheses fascinates me. Black and white never interest me but it is the grey that captivates me. I believed, for an extremely long time, that these personal preferences had much to do with my disdain for science. Science was always presented as a complete and already perfected field of study; I was taught to memorize what others had discovered without being offered explanations of what they had mistakenly tried or how they could have possibly known that an atom is made up of electrons, protons, and neutrons (is that even correct?). It seemed like there was no place in this world of scientific thought for someone like me, who thought in terms of "perhaps but not really" or "it could be, but then again it might not."

However, lately my opinion has begun to change. I have begun to question whether indeed science is flawless, and if it is indeed an imperfect field, then perhaps there is a place for me in it. In a world where we tend to rely so heavily on the phrase "scientifically proven," I have begun to doubt and question the importance of that term. Perhaps science only seems so flawless because the lay person is not placed in a position where he or she can actively and persuasively debate the merits of the findings.

CONSIDERING OPPOSING VIEWS

Connie E. Pearcy

Although I react violently to claims of objectivity by others, I think I often view my perspective as a superior perspective if not *the* superior perspective. Of course I would deny any chauvinism if questioned. And in theory I recognize the limits to my explanations of the world. In practice, however, my idealism often gives way to a closed-minded disregard of those who disagree with my philosophy (especially on issues of feminist criticism). How then can I remain convinced that what I do and how I see social reality contains meaning, while at the same time sincerely consider opposing views worthy of examination?

THE QUESTION OF STANDARDS

Amy C.

I find it quite difficult to evaluate my thoughts on the relationship between feminism and philosophy. If I try to use the standards I've learned, then of course most types of feminism do not "count" as philosophy, since it is precisely the standards that are in question. But then what standards do you use? I've pretty much learned to rely on my own intuitions and on those of some other students whom I trust. And to find literature that may help. And it's not that I want standards so that I can write off "bad" philosophy and thus be assured that my work is fine; but it's more that I think that if feminist knowledge is to "advance," then it has to be self-critical. It's just that it's hard to be self-critical when you simultaneously have to be on the defensive, knowing that plenty of people are critical, and not necessarily in your best interest. I haven't written a dissertation proposal yet, that comes sometime next spring. I don't know if I'll do a "feminist dissertation" or not; mostly because I'm not all that sure what one is. And I mean this sincerely. The problem is, however, not that this bothers me. I'm perfectly willing to embark on a project to see what sort of feminist critique could be made of a certain tradition in philosophy (personal identity). But the problem is that such a project would probably be ruled out as in principle not possible. That such a critique would not be possible. Since the project challenges standards, it has to be justified beforehand. The issue of "standards"—as if standards are not set by particular groups of people with particular interests, but rather are pre-given and unchallengeable—is probably the single most important issue that I have to face. It's probably the same for most feminist-type graduate students. It's the old "respectability" issue in its contemporary academic dress.

RIPPLING EFFECTS

Elana Newman

I know that as a psychology student with weaknesses in my historical understanding of my field and the discipline, I have often felt alienated and off track in the course. Particularly at the beginning, I felt far off at sea, indulgent in taking this course not directly tied to my work. It was not initially clear to me what I could bring to my discipline from the historical analysis. I feel that my lack of knowledge about what other disciplines actually grapple with prevented me from at times fully appreciating some of the material. . . . Although I felt this alienation and interdisciplinary dilemma acutely, I also feel that creating my own path and struggling with how to claim the material as my own was useful. It was frightening at times to think I was wasting my resources, doubting my intellectual integrity, etc., but realizing I had some intellectual resources in the end was exciting. So the ambivalence about interdisciplinary and home discipline work may have been very productive.

I have found that my confidence in considering feminist issues and raising them less defensively in my department has altered. Senior faculty members are willing to engage with me, and I feel more equipped analytically to pursue these conversations. I am more likely to admit my doubts and my convictions about the way gender is handled in the field. I think much of this has been reinforced by my mentor's simultaneously growing more articulate about and theoretically grounded in feminist psychology.

A side benefit I noted was not only a growing critique of my field but growing appreciation for my field, and the academics over in the psychology department. As my colleagues became more rebellious about the home front, I found myself more able to appreciate my faculty and colleagues. Surprisingly I found myself engaging with faculty about my intellectual struggles with gender and opening new avenues for discussion with them. In my teaching, gender was incorporated with the curriculum naturally and at a higher level of analysis than previously. I feel like my thoughts and struggles have had small rippling effects in my department, which is quite satisfying.

SIX

Learning about Sexual
Harassment and Rape

> More than rape itself, the fear of rape permeates our
> lives. And what does one do from day to day, with *this*
> experience, which says, without words and directly to
> the heart, *your existence, your experience may end at
> any moment?* Your experience may end, and the best
> defense against this is not to be, to deny being . . . to . . .
> avert your gaze, make yourself, as a presence in the
> world, less felt.—Susan Griffin, as quoted in Adrienne
> Rich, *On Lies, Secrets, and Silence*

We begin this section with Susan Griffin's quote because it names the
subtle psychic collusion between what we call the petty coercions and
the grand exclusions. This is not to say that sexual harassment and rape
are petty coercions—no, not petty at all. But the many ways in which
we, as women, try to defend ourselves from them, by making ourselves
(in Griffin's words) "less felt," suggest that no moment of self-reflection
is too small or too unimportant to be left untouched by the coercions.
The coercions operate at an internalized, emotional level. They are deeply
and thoroughly felt. Thus testimonies show that those who experience
rape/sexual harassment, no matter the circumstances, wonder if they are
complicit, wonder whether their concerns have meaning or moral value.

An awareness of how sexual harassment and rape shape women's lives
has been at the core of women's studies since its beginnings. Political out-
rage over rape shaped the early women's movement, and marshaling legal
resources to combat sexual harassment continues to be a primary activist
concern. Courses in women's studies, in both the interdisciplinary and
disciplinary forms, discuss the sexual objectification of women as a pervasive quality of contemporary life. Threat of sexual harassment and rape
remains a constant in women's experiences, and attention to it is central
to feminist consciousness and feminist theory about those experiences.[1]

However pervasive the awareness of violence against them is, and however pervasive its discussion in women's studies classes, individual women students probably do not first encounter sexual harassment and rape as subject matter within a theoretical framework. Long before they come into a women's studies classroom, they have confronted unwanted male attention within the family, in the workplace, or on a date. They may not have yet learned the crucial lesson that rape and sexual harassment are about power, not about sexuality.

The readings in this section self-reflectively recount contributors' individual stories about violence against women in the process of learning about theoretical perspectives on it.[2] Ginger Brent's contribution considers the notion that women are at least in part to blame for the sexist environment in which they live. After all, there are certain advantages to learned helplessness. Someone else will change your flat tire, or carry that heavy box, or let you have the first turn in line. So, you have only yourself to blame if men do not think of you as an equal. It is a healthy beginning point in the sense that it suggests that women must be a presence in the world in order even to imagine the possibility of change. Contributions by Elizabeth Sayre and Laura M. also take up the complicity theme, in particular as it reveals a collusion between racism and a feminist perspective and as it complicates efforts to define sexual harassment.

In a detailed account of a specific relationship, Laura M. identifies the behavior, situations, and power dynamics that made her uncomfortable—that discouraged her intellectual interest in her chosen field because she was unwilling to be a part of the relationship as it seemed to be defined by her professor; because she was unwilling to be harassed, to experience the uncomfortableness. Yet, in the end, she questions herself, even so; her silence, she thinks, means that she was partly to blame. Just having to think about it, she tells us, is a drain. It feels like a lose-lose situation.

The contribution by Jennifer L. is a still more detailed account, this time describing the events surrounding an attempted rape. It is a remarkable story because it uncovers how social practices such as the "dinner-dance-overnight" can create a climate for sexual harassment and attempted rape. Jennifer L. responded to the situation not by blaming herself for agreeing to go on the date, but by refusing to be silenced. She insisted that the problem was not only with an individual but with the environment in which men lived. It was a problem that needed the attention of the men who were responsible for it. It was a problem whose remedy lay with those who perpetuated it.

The last two entries, one by a woman and one by a man, are about how (or if) most American men can understand the full impact of a culture of rape and sexual harassment. The contributors do not agree on this, but both make it clear that men, too, are now asking, "Am I a part of the problem?" This is a step in the right direction.

WHO'S RESPONSIBLE?

Ginger Brent

I often wonder how often I provoke sexist responses. I am not only referring to those times when I stand by my car looking helpless knowing that if I look that way some man will come along and change my tire, but when I arrive to stand in line at approximately the same time as two guys and allow the man behind the counter to wait on me first because I'm a woman, or even when I smile differently at men (in a way that's younger, somehow) than I do at women. The problem is that sometimes I notice what I'm doing while I'm doing it, but don't stop; and sometimes I don't notice it until I think about it later. On those occasions when I notice what I'm doing but don't stop it's because I'm being pragmatic (maybe even saving time so that I can get home and think about my women's studies journal entries!); when I don't notice it I guess it's because I've learned certain lessons about male and female behavior so well that it's hard to unlearn them. At any rate, my own behavior prevents me from being as outraged as some about the vagueness of this university's definitions of sexual harassment, and as sure of who's responsible for it.

WHEN I'M ALONE ON THE STREET

Elizabeth S. Sayre

You hear a lot of informed, feminist women talking about how 75 percent of rapes happen between people who know each other, and most happen between people of the same race, but in my own mind and in many other people's, too, date rape or rape between people who know each other, between people of the same race, is something we never hear about in newspaper stories. . . . I think date and acquaintance rape probably are much less visible because women blame themselves in these situations and are unsure about what constitutes sexual violation. It's much easier [if you're white] to fear and hate the imaginary black stranger than it is to say that [a fraternity brother] raped you. I am not innocent of those ideas either, although I have certainly not been date-raped and none of my friends have told me if they have been. But when I'm alone on the street at night (as little as possible now that I've started thinking about it more—I got a ride home from Public Safety this week and felt very strange, like I was riding in an armored car with authorities of the State, which I guess I was, like I was cheating thanks to my privilege, or something), black men make me more nervous than white. . . . I hate that. It's horrible. I don't want it to be that way. It seems like I have a lot of awareness of problems, but few ways to deal with them. . . . Maybe that's why I feel paralyzed a lot of the time?? Or maybe I'm just inventing an excuse here.

THE LITTLE THINGS THAT DRAG YOU DOWN

Laura M.

During my first two years in our program, a professor had high hopes (I think) that I would become his protégée. This professor always searches amongst the new students to try to find a protégée. It's kind of an inside joke amongst the graduate students, since there have been four consecutive incoming classes where someone was selected out as the possible protégée. Now this person is very paternalistic, and rigorous, and reflective, and all that, and so is intimidating to many people, not just students. I was never intimidated by him, not that I can remember. I did well in his classes, and he thought I was bright and had good intuitions, etc. But, and I really disliked this, he couldn't help but "steal" glances at my breasts when talking to me (usually when I was talking to him), and then when I had an independent study with him, I had to do problems on his blackboard and would feel uncomfortable as hell, with him sitting behind me. I don't know if he was leering or not, it doesn't matter; his general behavior of always taking notice of my breasts was enough to make me uncomfortable with him sitting there. Now I've had men stare at my breasts all my life, since I've had noticeable ones for most of my life; so I'm used to the general phenomenon. However, this is supposed to be someone concerned with what I'm *thinking*, someone with whom I might enter into a student-teacher one-on-one relationship. How are you supposed to trust someone who's always got to look at your breasts, someone who is paternalistic and self-righteous to boot? So I decided that he was repressed and lecherous. His specialization is OK, but I couldn't devote my life to it, so this is probably not the greatest disaster ever to befall me. But the point is that this sort of thing has a definite effect on how well you can function as a graduate student; you find yourself forced to be self-conscious about something that really shouldn't be an issue.

Now what I've started thinking about, besides how much I resented it at the time (this professor no longer really speaks to me much; I guess I made it clear that I wasn't interested in working with him, although he probably believes that it's because I've rejected the subject area, when that's not really the case; it had to do more with him than the subject matter), was that at the time I considered it a form of sexual harassment, though not one explicitly listed anywhere. It would be very hard to have this sort of thing recognized as sexual harassment. And I'm not sure that I think it should be, in that this might not be the sort of thing that I would want someone to be "punished" or "reprimanded" for. But then I think that if this sort of thing is not recognized, then what little chance there is of reducing such behavior will never be realized. And I still wonder, should I have "called" him on this, and just said, Please stop looking at my breasts when we're having a conversation. He would have been shocked, I'm sure; he probably has no idea that he's as lecherous as he is, and being very religious, he would probably have taken great offense. But I felt like saying it then, and I guess I feel I should have. Now the fact that this is such a big deal, should I have brought it up or not, indicates to me that something is already wrong. Why is it that we get into these weird power relations where you can't just say to someone, "You're treating me badly," if you feel that they are. Anyway, it just started me thinking about all the "little" things that drag you down day to day.

MISUSE OF POWER

Beth H.

The issue of what constitutes sexual harassment has currently become a covert, not openly discussed, topic in my department. One of my male colleagues who has been teaching undergraduates has been the focus of many rumors about inappropriate boundaries with students and to my understanding he has been confronted in a less than satisfactory way. Apparently fellow students filed complaints, based on rumor. Recently some of my students have indicated that they had friends in his class who felt harassed on some level. Although some of it seems sexual, it also seems that students are frightened by his use of power, intellectually as a tool. And I have started discussing with him (in a nonthreatening manner) teaching techniques and the issue of power. Ultimately it has challenged me to redefine misuse of power and think about how one might experience powerful teachers as men and women in the academy. Incidentally, I never realized how truly faulty prominent legal codes are—what might appear to be gains for women may actually be hindrances. For example, I had always thought this university and my professional association had triumphed in naming and defining sexual harassment as an issue. Unfortunately I did not recognize that the "deliberate, intentional, and repeated" clause excluded passing sexist comments from scrutiny.

FRATERNITY SPRING FORMAL

Jennifer L.

During one recent weekend I had the dubious pleasure of attending the annual spring formal of one of the most notorious fraternities on campus. A member of my sorority set me up with a friend of hers who needed a date, and I went feeling excited to go and have a good time, but also feeling a bit anxious, knowing full well that group's horrible reputation as slime balls and perverts. However, I felt confident enough in my own strength to not let anything I didn't want to happen happen, and anyway—those rumors could have been all hearsay.

Unfortunately, my experience at the formal turned out to be one of the biggest nightmares of my life. And after talking with many of the other women who had gone, most of them members of my sorority or one of a few others, I discovered that my experience was not a unique one—to a lesser or even greater degree, other women had similar encounters the same night. The entire fraternity and their dates inhabited three floors of a hotel (two hours from here, so an overnight stay was mandatory). It was so obvious to me, walking through the halls at the end of the night, that every male was trying his hardest to get his date back into their room to "hook up," and every female was trying her hardest to avoid doing just that. As I went from a cocktail party to dinner to the dance and finally to the hotel after the dance, the whole scene grew more and more repugnant to my eyes.

There was a lot of alcohol involved, as there is at most functions on campus, and my date happened to be one of the heaviest drinkers in the group. Starting during dinner, he began to make overt sexual advances at me which I found grossly insulting and slowly but surely ruined my night. I spent hours all night long trying to avoid him and find help from a friend, but I was really on my own. I dreaded going back to the hotel, knowing that a private room was waiting for us upon our return (which surprised me a lot—considering I had just met this guy only a few hours before).

My date began to frighten me. After failing to reject him subtly and politely, I resorted to other tactics—I was plain rude to him repeatedly, thinking to myself, "How could this guy be so persistent? Can't he tell that I'm *not* interested?" As the evening progressed, he just became more aggressive and forceful. My fear increased and I began to feel desperate, wanting only to go home to my dorm room with a locked door. I at last broke down, and burst into tears out of desperation, when my date asked me, grabbing my wrist, showing off his prowess in front of all his friends, to "suck his shotgun" later in the evening. I had always hoped to be strong enough in a situation like that to be able to come back with a smart re-mark and blow him off, but all I could do was cry. And his friends just laughed—no sympathy or concern at all.

I thought about calling a taxi and driving home, but I realized that I had no money. There was no one to call, and most everyone there at the dance was either already back at the hotel with their boyfriends or too drunk to help me out anyway. I sat in the bathroom for a long time, and soon found a friend of mine who was not surprisingly in a situation similar to mine, although her date was a friend of hers. We agreed to go back to the hotel together and not to leave each other alone until we were "safe." So we gathered our dates and left for the hotel.

Back at the hotel, I changed into my sweats in the locked bathroom, hoping that my date was drunk enough to pass out while I was out of sight. Unfortunately, I came out of the bathroom to find him sprawled over one bed, naked, apparently waiting for me. I wasn't scared anymore—now I was angry. I ignored him and got into the other bed, picking up the phone to call my friend and tell her to come and save me. But he took the phone from my hand, and proceeded to tell me about how much he was in love with me, how badly he wanted to have sex with me, and how unfair it was to come all the way out there with him and not sleep in his bed. I thought I was going to be sick. I tried to ignore him and answer all his questions and comments with monotone replies, but it didn't work. All of a sudden he was lying in bed next to me, and his hands were everywhere. I was absolutely terrified—too terrified to do anything but lie there and hope he was only kidding and would soon stop. But he didn't—instead he grabbed both of my arms and pinned them down above my head with one hand, and pulled my boxer shorts down with the other. It was at that moment that I realized my danger. If I didn't do something soon, I was going to be raped. So, I began to kick and plead with him to stop, and finally, he stood up and got off the bed, the terror on my face being I think the only thing to stop him. "You really don't want to do this, huh?" he said. I got up and quickly walked out of the room, heading for my friend's room down the hall where a large group of people were watching a movie. I stayed there until after five o'clock in the morning, and when I finally went back to our room, my date was fast asleep, passed out.

The next day, I woke up still very frightened and feeling disgusting. My date was extremely hung over, and seemed to have no memory of his sick behavior the night before (or if he did, he didn't consider it to be anything out of the ordinary). I was so uncomfortable for the rest of the day, feeling a bit too close to being an actual rape victim for comfort. I only began to feel better about it after talking to some friends, and discovering that they too had had to fight off their dates the same night. One girl was with her boyfriend and was coerced into having sex with him when she really had no desire to all night, and another had been in a situation like mine, but not quite as forceful. One more girl had gone with a blind date, like me, and had spent the night with a girlfriend on another floor, for fear of being trapped in a room with her drunken date. It was horrifying to me that so many females had been in such demeaning circumstances and could only complain about it.

I decided that the only place to start in this situation would be to talk to people—guys I thought I could count on to be sympathetic and girls I thought would be outraged. But people's responses to my story ranged from remarks like "Oh, give him a break, he was pretty drunk" to "The poor guy hasn't had it in so long—you should have shown him a good time" to "Why didn't you just relax and enjoy it? It couldn't have been all that bad." Feeling violated and almost contaminated by my experience, I could only excuse the reactions on the grounds that they must not know how it felt. It was extremely disappointing to me that so many of my sorority sisters were so willing to pass off his behavior as "drunken stupidity" or "his sick sense of humor." However, there were a few people who shared my disgust and anger, and they were willing to listen to my grievances and understand them.

Fortunately, in my situation, I had someone who was willing to help me to try to change things. One of my friends, who was dating a member of my date's fraternity, sat down with me, her boyfriend, and the fraternity president, and we discussed just what had happened and the consequences of the actions. I was impressed to see the two men take the situation very seriously, and they apologized on behalf of their brother, my date. But I didn't want an apology—I wanted them to do something about their pledge class. I suggested that the president sit down with all of the pledges at a meeting and discuss with them the seriousness of sexual harassment, the respect they should hold for any woman whom they happen to meet or date on campus and everywhere, and point out to them the alarming statistics on acquaintance rape in our society. I even offered to do the discussion myself, but because it would be a fraternity function, I wouldn't be allowed to attend. They did promise me that they would sit down with my date personally and chat with him in addition to the promised "rape workshop" with the pledges.

At this point, I am happy that I was able to convey my concern and anger to at least two members of the fraternity, and that they took it seriously enough to do something about it. Whether it will ever happen or not before the end of the semester is questionable, but at least now the fraternity knows that not every woman on campus is going to blow off gross behavior such as that displayed by one member to me that night, and by other members to other women that night and probably every night. The campus-wide activity and growing awareness of the problem of rape is also encouraging to see. Someday women might not have to spend an entire evening on their guard or fight off a mere acquaintance, a good friend, or a stranger who tried to force them into sexual acts.

POWER STRUGGLE

Liz Morgan

I don't know if men can ever really understand rape. I have had several men come to me in the past few years telling me that they have just discovered that a woman whom they know was raped, either recently or in the past. My first reaction is that they know many women who have been raped, and they just aren't aware of it, citing my "one in four women will be sexually assaulted by the time they are thirty" statistic. In both cases of stranger or acquaintance rape, these men are initially angry at the rapist, but then they tell me that they just don't know how to treat the victim. They are embarrassed to talk to her at all, much less about the rape, because they feel like they know something they shouldn't, even if she told them herself. I try to explain that at this awful time in her life, the last thing a woman needs is for her friends to feel uneasy around her. This will only make her feel more responsible and ashamed than she already does. These men still see rape as a shameful thing, I suppose because of our Victorian ideas about sex as being dirty. I don't think they understand the power struggle involved.

LOCKER-ROOM LANGUAGE

Michael W. Ruiz

Possibly the most difficult issue I will be acting upon for the rest of my life is that dealing with rape language. Many of the terms and phrases I have used in my life fall squarely into this category. I don't feel the need to describe which terminology I place where, but I do see the use of such language as detrimental. It will be hard to enter a "locker-room" situation and speak up against the use of rape language. That will be one of many situations I will encounter, but I fear the numbing effect such language has on the brain more. I am still infuriated that adult men and women could release a rapist because his victim wasn't wearing underwear, or that college men only believe rape is rape when you come out from behind a tree and attack a total stranger. I am not willing to belong to that mindset, but neither do I wish to do nothing about it. It won't be easy.

1. See, e.g., Susan Brownmiller's *Against Our Will* (New York: Bantam Books, 1976); Bernice Lott, Mary Ellen Reilly, and Dale R. Howard, "Sexual Assault and Harassment: A Campus Community Case Study," *Signs* 8, no. 2 (Winter 1982): 296–319; and Diana E. H. Russell, *Sexual Exploitation: Rape, Child Sexual Abuse, and Sexual Harassment* (Beverly Hills, Calif.: Sage, 1984).

2. A comparison of three major introductory women's studies texts illustrates the range of theoretical perspectives available: in Jo Freeman's *Women*, 4th ed. (Mountain View, Calif.: Mayfield, 1989), rape and sexual harassment are topics that (along with abortion and women's health concerns) come under the umbrella issue of women's control of their own bodies; in Sheila Ruth's *Issues in Feminism*, 2d ed. (Mountain View, Calif.: Mayfield, 1990), rape is introduced as the biological imperative of patriarchy, as "man's basic weapon of force against woman, the principal agent of his will and her fear" (177); and in Virginia Sapiro's *Women in American Society* (Mountain View, Calif.: Mayfield, 1986), rape and sexual harassment are presented as both perpetrating and perpetuating a series of social myths built on an adversarial ideology of sexuality (303).

SEVEN

Thinking about
Sexuality, Reproduction, and Abortion

Abortion—Is a form of punishment for the crime of wishing not to be pregnant. (Adrienne Rich, *Of Woman Born*, 265–69)

Heterosexuality—A sexual feeling for a person (or persons) of the opposite sex, a feeling experienced and enjoyed by some women and some men.

Homophobia—The fear of feelings of love for members of one's own sex and therefore the hatred of those feelings in others. (Audre Lorde, *Sister Outsider: Essays and Speeches*, 45)

Lesbian—A social identification of a woman-identified woman. A concept which causes many people discomfort.

Orgasm—Feeling of intense sexual pleasure as the vagina goes into rhythmic muscular contractions . . . May be repeated indefinitely . . . a total body experience.

—cited in Cheris Kramarae and Paula A. Treichler, *A Feminist Dictionary*

In American culture, sexuality is a currency that, if you are male, buys you success, envy, and good health. If you are female, sexuality buys you loss of status and, should you get pregnant, moral and economic crisis. Despite twenty years of feminist scholarship pointing out the debilitating effects of this double standard on women's sexual desire, and despite increases in sexual activities, sexual relations for campus women of the 1990s are fraught with guilt and ambivalence. Yet, it is an ambivalence born of subtleties, not naivete. Orgasm, birth control, compulsory heterosexuality, reproductive choice, lesbian identity: yes, these students are discussing intimately personal issues; no, they do not have any answers, for themselves or for others. The readings in this section do not celebrate new sexual freedoms, nor do they explore sexual desire or fantasy. They

97

focus on obstacles, on the interruptions, on the difficulties of having a sexual life at all.

THE CLITORIS

Deborah K. Chappel

I lived many years not knowing the clitoris existed. I remember the vague drawings in high school biology—I know the vagina was there, but I feel pretty sure the clitoris wasn't or we'd have wondered about it among ourselves. It's like, then, a part of me was simply excised from the picture. Female pleasure was put on a "need to know" basis, and somebody must have thought we didn't need to know very much about it at all. Not then, when Saturday night petting promised what was never delivered; not later, when vaginal intercourse didn't deliver that much either (the song "Is That All There Is?" comes to mind). I didn't talk about it, mostly because I assumed there was something wrong with me. Years later, when I finally started figuring it out, I was angry—at the men or boys who didn't know or care, the culture which made it so difficult to find out, even my own body which had hidden its secrets from me.

When I worked at a law office there was an older woman (sixty-five to seventy years) who'd been injured and had to undergo a complete physical for the insurance company. When the report came back, everyone passed it around and sniggered. It read, "Vaginal examination could not be completed. Opening will not admit the tip of index finger." It had grown closed! She'd spent her whole life as a virgin. None of us, in the decade following the sexual revolution, could believe it. Yet at that time, and after a couple of years of marriage, I didn't know about the clitoris, and I hadn't experienced the *big o* either. She may have known more about her own body than I did.

Think clitoris, Shulman says.

HETEROSEXIST THINKING

Mary R. Bowman

I am very committed to the acceptance of homosexuality and the validation of gay people and their perspectives and experiences, but at the same time I know that as a heterosexual woman in this society I am prone to heterosexist thinking and attitudes, and I can't pretend to have completely eradicated them already. Because I'm aware of that, it really bothers me to disagree with gay people when they are discussing gay issues. Yet some things I do strongly disagree with. "Lesbians are women who survive without men financially and emotionally, representing the ultimate in an independent life-style," they declare proudly. Yet they also remind us that a woman may be a lesbian "concurrently with marriage," a contradiction with the previous statement, and more importantly they imply that any lesbian, even if emotionally or financially dependent, or both, on a *woman* is nevertheless more independent than any given heterosexual woman. "Lesbians are the women who battle day by day to show that women are valid human beings, not just appendages of men," they claim, and that definite article implies that no heterosexual women are engaged in that day-to-day battle. These are more examples of some people being valorized but at the cost of belittling others—here heterosexual feminists. Some of my best friends are heterosexual feminists. The same is true of the curious insistence that lesbians outnumber gay men. And that lesbians have it worse in this society. How would a gay man like that? Some of my best friends are gay men. Other things: the locating of the origin of sexism in "making reproduction rather than personal pleasure or personal development the goal of sexual intercourse" struck me as odd. They could be right, I'll admit, but this is a claim I don't think I've heard before, and they just assert it, they don't argue it. That's certainly a *feature* of sexist attitudes, but the sole cause? I'm not convinced. And heterosexual intercourse is necessarily oppressive: "No matter what the feminist does, the physical act throws man and woman back into role playing: the male as conqueror asserts his masculinity and the female is expected to be a passive receiver." Again, this isn't exactly a hopeful or an approbating message to heterosexual women.

Anyway, I've just been enumerating some of the things that made me feel torn, ambivalent, to try to see if I can make sense of the repeated occurrences of that experience. I'm not sure I have. Part of the reason, I think, is that I feel emotionally and intellectually committed to the cause, and so I can't let disagreement be total and simple. But why is there as much disagreement as there is?

PREMARITAL COPULATION

Reid Smith

From my perspective in the 1980s, it is difficult to conceive (pardon) of not having birth control. Not using any dominated my first sexual relationship. Even with my significant other using the pill, the question of whether it's working constantly looms in the background.

I didn't grow up with any notion that "premarital copulation" (term borrowed from a Tennessee police officer when I was stopped while driving with an ex-girlfriend back to college) was immoral—only dangerous. Ignorance of the female body as well as my own was terrifying, but a much more oppressive fear was that I would get someone pregnant.

When I was in high school and the first three years of college, an unwanted pregnancy would have meant an unwanted abortion—something I neither wanted for my partner nor for my guilty conscience. Now, were my girlfriend to get pregnant, the consequences would have an even greater effect upon our lives.

Because abortion would be a completely unsatisfactory form of de facto birth control, we would commit ourselves to living hell. Yet, Margaret Sanger is still right on the money many decades later with her assertion that birth control is a woman's problem. I, personally, do not view it as such—repeatedly, I have been willing to take fewer risks than my partners. (This is probably a result of having a mother who constantly harped on the subject plus a healthy appreciation for my responsibility in the event of conception.) The very fact that I have had to convince women that it was in our mutual interests to go out to the drugstore attests to the fact that women, first, need to become more conscious of the necessity of birth control, before men as a group accept this responsibility. It is endemic in our society for men to consider the consequences of sex as the female's problem. While it may be placing an unfair burden on women to be responsible, nature has also, unfairly perhaps, imbued them with the consequences of sexual intercourse.

When women, as a group, embrace contraceptive measures as a necessity to equality, men will also realize this.

GETTING PREGNANT

Martha P.

I was thinking today about all the rapes that have been committed on campus in the past two days, and on the issue of abortion. Actually, I was thinking about the way I conceptualize my own sexual identity—but let's leave that on a back burner for the moment. Thinking about the fact that prolife people would legalize abortion if a woman had been raped, I realized that the dispute about abortion is actually a dispute about the status of women in our society, and their right as individuals to experience sexual pleasure; that is, that women are being required to think of their sexuality only in procreative terms—that they should have sex for no other reason than to have children, and that all other behavior is deemed deviant or illicit. Why else would a woman have sex if not for production, seems to be the argument; only when she is taken against her will is she freed from all responsibility and her choice to kill the fetus left open. But how is this argument prolife? It's downright hypocritical! Women are being told that they are to have *responsible* sex, that intercourse should not be a pleasurable activity in and of itself but should only be indulged in for the sake of having children and increasing the social store. Women are being viewed as objects for production rather than (sexual) human *subjects*.

I still don't think I could have an abortion. And I wonder about the way my feelings about abortion have served to limit my own sexual behavior/ exploration. Control has always been a big issue in my life, and controlling my body has obviously played a role. But it has affected me to the point where for a time I decided to abstain from intercourse for fear of getting pregnant and the contingent fear that my life would thereby fall apart. What I am getting at is that I question the way certain socially transmitted (diseases) lessons have served to limit my freedom, to oppress me rather than to liberate me—it was just as unacceptable for me to have an abortion as to bear a child out of wedlock, before my career was established, before I was economically independent. So while abortion was out of the question—psychologically, emotionally—so was the possibility of getting pregnant at the wrong time, by the wrong man: the prescriptions of right and wrong having been inculcated from the time I could understand what sex and its consequences were. By concentrating on the potential consequences of sleeping with a man, by focusing on conception, I thought the way to stay in control, to exercise my right to self-determination, was simply to stay out of bed—to not allow myself to be seduced by the clever lover.

I am now beginning to have a different understanding of the whole scenario. I understand how I have been depriving myself of my own sexuality, of my own body, and my own human subjectivity. I had thought in the past that the notion of "getting pregnant at the wrong time" was wrong—that there was no such thing as the wrong time; that if one wanted a child, no time could be termed "wrong" by conventional dictums. There might be more opportune times (economically speaking, professionally, emotionally), but I resented the fact that I should be made to feel ashamed of the fact that I was carrying a child. I have since had several friends who have had abortions. Some dealt with it as just another shot in the arm—a fact of life. And I can honestly say, at least now, that I have no trouble with that attitude. I, however, identify more with a friend who experienced a deep depression, a tremendous sense of guilt and shame and failure, and who attempted suicide. She is from a very traditional Catholic family, and was brought up in a very strict household, although I am not sure why these details should matter. In any case, I can see the same thing happening to me if I were ever in her situation—I don't think I could deal with the sense of failure, because pregnancy has always been so tied up for me with this issue of being in control, which in turn is fundamental to my sense of self-respect.

But (and this is a biggie)—now I wonder: am I more in control when I abstain or when I allow my desires free rein; when I allow myself to feel desire or when I keep my body and emotions in check for fear of where they may lead me? It's not an easy question. I think it's a matter of weighing things carefully in my mind. Of recognizing the role society has played in legitimizing a particular time for a particular act (sex/birth), and how that time may be incompatible with my own. And that it's OK. That the consequences are all mine—although society also plays a role (discrimination against the single mother, for example; we're still at this stage, aren't we?).

I know I've been talking as though there were no such thing as birth control. I guess I have a hard time trusting its effectiveness. I know there are other issues involved in my own sexual subjectivity—issues equally tied up with my notions of self-respect, integrity, "femininity," parental expectations, etc.—but this debate about abortion has set me thinking about my own experience, about how large a role society and fear can play in a woman's psyche, and especially in one seeking social approbation, wanting to "perform" according to the expectations raised around her. And this has as much to do with the women's lib movement as with our friendly patriarch handing the law down from on high. I want to begin thinking of myself as a subject—that while I have done so in my work, in literary analysis, while I have broached these issues through literature, it is much harder to apply the same terms to my own life. And I need to start doing that. I want to start doing that. Particularly in this issue involving self-control. That self-control does not mean deprivation. This just seems utterly wrong.

MY BEST FRIEND'S ABORTION

Sarah G.

It is one of the most difficult memories of my life, and I'm not even certain that I can call it a mere memory, for seldom does a week—or even a day— pass when at some point I do not reflect on the decision my high school friend made when she chose at age sixteen to have an abortion. We were in the same first-grade class; she still lives six houses from mine. She had dated her boyfriend since the ninth grade, and after her sweet sixteen birthday party, she and he made love for the first time. My friend's mother would have died had she known; hers is an intensely religious family, and although her older sister had married just out of high school, her parents had other plans for her: college, medical school, and a great career were their goals for their daughter. But she was in love with her boyfriend, and for one evening her passion overcame her "plans" and she was left with an unexpected complication—a baby was growing inside of her.

She came to me because she had no other place to turn. She was scared to death and totally confused. She had yet to even tell her boyfriend, and she never did—an act which to this day haunts me. Ultimately, the decision to abort was hers, but—initially—she consulted me when she should have been speaking with the father of her unborn child. I was so frightened for her; I could not believe that she was pregnant, and really did not know how to help her. I just tried to listen and be there for her, because we both knew that she faced but one legitimate alternative, and that was to abort the fetus she carried. Her mother could never know about the baby. And so, she went to a private clinic and underwent an abortion.

These experiences surged to the fore of my mind after reading about the abortion issue for class. This is a difficult issue in feminist politics—it is really especially difficult to reconcile emotionally, ethically, and politically. . . . My problem with abortion stems from some pretty traditional values that I hold to be important as I lead my life. I'm far from prudish, but I do feel that "making love" has been demoralized in our society. It no longer means to so many people what it somehow means to me: the most intimate and special act that two people can share as they realize their love for one another. Now, sex is not often interpreted in this manner, and it continues to follow that *all* of the responsibility for birth control falls upon the woman. As abortion has spread, there has been increased pressure upon women to abort unplanned children. This is unfair, for the woman is so put upon in this society. At the same time, however, a woman should retain the right to control her body, and hence, the choice to abort must be made available to her.

I disagree with the assumption that feminists should not grieve after undergoing an abortion merely because they are termed "feminist." This is silly. I feel that it would be wholly unnatural for a woman *not* to grieve after an abortion, and that grief would not invalidate a woman's claim as a feminist in any way. I also disagree that abortion is a means for a woman to "gain control" of her life. Perhaps this woman could have gained control *before* the unwanted pregnancy by saying "no" or by ensuring that she and her partner were using proper methods of birth control. Of course, if she can be comfortable with her decision to abort, then it is perhaps a means of earning control. I do agree that there must exist improved communication between adversaries on this issue. I myself am guilty of harboring great anger and frustration at the inane tactics of prolifers, who refuse to look to the heart of the matter to see that abortion is *not* at all an easy decision and yet it is an absolutely necessary choice for women to have. If somehow this hostile relationship could be alleviated, there would be a far greater chance to reach laws amenable to women's reality in the 90s. And as difficult as it is, abortion must remain a safe and viable option for women unable to care for a baby, or for women who wish not to carry to term. As for sex selection—*No!* I have a hard time accepting the termination of a pregnancy solely based on parents' wishes to deliver a boy or a girl.

Whatever happened to my friend? Not much. Her boyfriend could never understand why she refused to be intimate with him after the period around her birthday when they were often together. And she could never return the relationship to how it had been before the "divorce" she imposed between them following her abortion. He was a constant reminder of the baby she never carried to term, and she couldn't deal with that. I couldn't deal with his questioning me about "what was wrong" with my friend. I hated the dishonesty, and I still do. She's now about to graduate from college, and she is dating a guy she began seeing last spring—her first since she was sixteen. Her mother never did learn of her abortion, but she is considering—strangely enough—telling her current boyfriend about her experience. Whether her deep depression was the result of her abortion or her breakup with her boyfriend, I am not certain, but I know that it was most likely a combination of both. Personally, I know I never want to face what she faced when she was but sixteen, nor what she continues to face each day as she wonders about what could have been had her pregnancy come two years later.

TALK ABOUT IT

Carole V.

Birth control may be legal, but in a large, real way we still aren't allowed to talk about it. One of the best things a liberated woman can do, I think, is to keep her own children very well informed about birth control and about choices, and hope they spread the word on the grapevine, since that is where kids get a lot of their information. In a small way, you can subvert the oppressive forces while working to get them removed. My mother got married without having any idea at all what sex was. At nineteen, I had some dim ideas, and then found out for certain for myself by experiment. I don't wish my daughter or son (if I have either) to grow up in ignorance. Women have a real responsibility to fight those who would impose their morality on others, because it usually translates to imposing it on women. That means, for me, even though I morally disapprove of abortion, I must fight to keep it legal because we are so, so far from an ideal world where it isn't necessary.

ABORTION

Heather H. Howard

The question of whether abortion should be easy for women to get or not really grabbed me this semester. I was forced to realize that abortion was not a clear-cut issue as I had always seen it. Sure, on the face of it, abortion should be legal and that's that. A woman should have reproductive freedom. Basically, I believe women will never have a chance at equality (and I guess underlying that is the question: at what price, or on whose terms, equality?) unless they have control of their bodies. Thus, abortion restriction becomes the ultimate interference.

I've struggled a lot with the place of sexuality in my life. I guess I would rather not have to deal with my sexuality—I want to be judged by my intellectual merits, and things like sex differences "get in the way." According to that reasoning, abortion is important because it allows a woman to lead a "normal" life—sexuality can be hidden, taken for granted, and taken care of with abortion. A woman can decide for herself when she is ready to disrupt her life and bear a child. Of course, though, we cannot ignore our sexuality as many of us try to do. Maybe if we women were more comfortable with our sexuality, we could openly practice whatever orientation we wanted. If contraception and education were not hindered, and abortion was freely obtainable, women would be unburdened of the many risks that just being a woman entails. Imagine such a world. Women would have more chance of success in business, planning a life with a partner, or simply being independent and single, and would not be as dependent on men. In many ways restrictions on abortion only keep women in the cycle of dependency, whether it be dependency on the back-alley doctor, on a father or boyfriend, or even on the welfare system of our patriarchy. . . . I think that the pure empowerment that abortion's legality offers will help many women feel more in control of their lives and that this will run over into other areas of our lives. . . . I know, however, that we cannot redress all of women's problems today with the right to abortion. But at least freedom of choice is a start, hopefully with many repercussions. (Maybe that's what all those prolifers are worried about.)

REDEFINING SEX

Cynthia L. Randall

If we see that "sex," as it was conceived then and now, is not a natural given as much as a male-defined, limited segment of the total range of sexual possibilities, the lack of female interest in sex becomes not just socially constructed (as opposed to natural) but a tool which works to men's advantage. If men think that women essentially don't enjoy sex, they are excused if they fail to satisfy women, or if they use women's bodies for their own pleasure rather than for mutual pleasure. Male sex can then be infantile—wholly selfish, providing instant gratification without responsibility—without seeming immature or abnormal.

As sex is still regarded essentially as intercourse which the man instigates, it is not surprising that the "sexual revolution" failed. Shulman wrote about the clitoris twenty years ago, and though the pill, which freed women to have sex for pleasure without procreative consequences, has become ubiquitous, the clitoris, which allows women to have sex for pleasure independent of intercourse, remains a hidden issue. Men have a clear stake in maintaining the idea that the penis is as essential for women as the vagina is for men. As sex is still essentially male-defined, women's increased access to it has not necessarily given us freedom or satisfaction. Even with the female orgasm an accepted phenomenon, men still expect women to have them as a result of penetration and women obligingly fake them to satisfy male egos—another indication that the sexual double standard works on more than one level.

What we need to do now is redefine sex to fit our experience, to reflect our priorities. The first step in this process, I think, is to recognize lesbian sex as a liberating part of feminism, as it demonstrates that the penis is not essential for female satisfaction and that there is a wide range of acts beyond intercourse which can be called "sex" and which can be complete in themselves. One reason men may be so afraid of lesbianism is that lesbians provide proof that women can live without men not just practically and emotionally but sexually. The penis is not primary. It is not as important to women as it is to men. It is essential for women to accept lesbianism, to recognize its importance for our movement, and to welcome not just its political but its sexual implications. Lesbianism is at the far end of a continuum of female freedom from male control, in all senses, and for heterosexuals to move forward on the continuum we need to see the full extent of possibility. Facing and accepting the validity of lesbian sex will help us redefine our own sexuality to correspond more accurately with our own needs and desires.

ALL RELATIONSHIPS ARE POLITICAL

Miriam Shadis

If lesbianism is more than sexual preference, it must be at least fundamentally partly sexual preference. Otherwise, if it was purely political, couldn't there (theoretically) be heterosexual lesbians? . . . Could a lesbian (a woman-identified woman) love a man? Can a man be woman-identified? I presume the answer would be no, but I don't see why not if it is a matter of politics—sexism is political, and that's why sexual preference matters at all. So if you get rid of sexism (for the sake of argument), then what happens—no lesbians, no heterosexuals, or just nobody cares? I guess I would accuse some lesbians of being a little sexist. Why should a woman choose her sister over her brother, all things being equal (they say never equal?). It seems to me that they're trying to get even with history, which I think is really silly.

I'm not even sure if the kind of lesbian relationship which lesbians seem to be projecting as an ideal can really work. It seems to me that all relationships are political, compromised by dependencies (which may alternate or vary in intensity). I guess the theory is that they aren't power based. But it has not been proved to me that power is inherently gendered. I'm sure that many lesbian relationships are based on power, or at least are not relationships between equally autonomous women. What I'm reacting to so strongly here is the notion that a feminist must be a lesbian. Ultimately I find that elitist and degrading to my culturally constructed, socialized little self.

WHAT'S AT STAKE

Alice Nelson

About the question of "choice" of heterosexuality—historically, there's really not been much of a "choice." This must be recognized; every social and cultural institution has demonstrated vested interests in reinforcing heterosexuality as the norm, and has marginalized those who did not "comply." The tricky part is that there appears not to be a way really to say, "I choose to be heterosexual." On the one hand, the response might be, "Are you *sure* you chose?" Well, no, I guess I'm not—but if I say I feel "naturally inclined" to be heterosexual, I run the risk of those nasty "it's unnatural to be homosexual" arguments that have historically been used as instruments to repress/oppress homosexuals. If I say yes, it still may be that I'm blind to the insidious forces that groomed my conformity as well as my fantasies, that no matter how I insist, it still may be that I haven't "seen the light," or that the most liberating experience may be the lesbian one. . . . *However*, and I think this is really the key, by making me go through this process of assessment and questioning, by making me declare my agency whatever my sexual preference, I must examine the political implications of my sexuality (and shaping my sexuality) in working for a transformative feminist agenda. In that sense, I could answer the question. In saying "I chose" I would be saying "I realize what's at stake."

LESBIAN RELATIONSHIPS AND POWER

Katie Kent

In their eagerness to point out the value and right of lesbianism to exist as an alternative to heterosexual love and marriage, and to participate in the women's movement, some feminists replicate precisely the same structures they are fighting against. Thus, they make lesbianism a sort of "magical sign," to borrow Katie King's phrase, a life-style that seems almost naturally feminist: lesbians are the most feminist; in fact, they were born that way. This is most apparent when they describe the early childhood years of a lesbian, and remark that she was always more conscious of sex-role stereotyping, that she rebelled against this, that, in other words, she had some sort of innate sense of what it means to be a feminist. However, feminist in this analogy comes to mean independent from men. While in some ways this is the goal of feminism, to gain psychic and physical independence from male/patriarchal dominance, it also ignores or subtly puts down the reality of heterosexual attachment for many women. This is a familiar tactic in lesbian writings (and in many writings by straight lesbian-wanna-be feminists)—they view the lesbian identity as somehow outside and exempt from the workings of heterosexual identity (while I, and many others, would argue that heterosexuality has a huge influence on and even control over my sexual identity as a lesbian) at the same time that they acknowledge and explicate the workings of patriarchy on society. Thus, they ignore both the difference of sexuality, and the validity of heterosexuality, at the same time that they try and deny the influence of heterosexuality on their own (lesbian) notions of identity. In other words, they argue that because we are lesbians we are outside the power plays involved in heterosexuality, and those women who are heterosexual are not really women in some sense, or at least not feminists. Lesbians are the authentic women, and lesbians are exempt from the problems faced by straight women. This idealized notion ignores, or blurs, the differences between lesbians themselves. Certainly, not all lesbians are feminists, and not all lesbians live feminist existences. Of course, as a lesbian I am often tempted to accept this analysis, and I do see it as a product of a specific moment in the women's movement, and also as a specific moment in the coming-out process for many women, the point at which you think of yourself as suddenly freed from all the old heterosexual games and power plays, liberated into another realm. However, there is just as much power floating around in lesbian relationships, whether acknowledged or not.

THE EASY WAY OUT

Elizabeth M.

I have often wondered how many women (including myself) are "heterosexual" not by choice or by compulsion but simply because they realize that it is the easy way out, that a lesbian existence is far, far more difficult to lead than a heterosexual one. To take an example from my own personal history: When I worked at a job I held after college, my co-worker was a lesbian. We soon became close friends, but it took her a long time to confide in me about her sexuality, and when she did, she was shaking. After all, such a confession could cost her not only my friendship (it didn't), but jeopardize her position in the company should I "blab" (I didn't). . . . After she had confided in me, I began to see through her eyes how difficult a lesbian existence could be, how much it relied on pretense and cover-up. Office politics almost required that we laugh and pretend we didn't mind when the men made sexist/condescending remarks or inquired into our private lives—"Do you have a boyfriend?"—and my friend was not very good at lying. What's more, while on the road or at conferences, all the employees were reimbursed for phone calls to their spouses or significant others, but my friend, who had had a long-time lover, never reported her calls because it would entail coming out to our boss, a risky move. Perhaps worst of all, once I began to socialize with her and her lover, I was shocked by the attitudes of strangers on the street. One time when we were leaving a restaurant, they began to hold hands. Almost immediately, a guy came up to us and spit on them, screaming "Fucking dykes!" at all three of us. I remember thinking at that moment how glad I was that I didn't have to undergo that sort of treatment on a daily basis, which led me to wonder whether my heterosexuality was more a matter of preference or of convenience. The verdict is still out.

EIGHT

Teaching Women's Studies

Striving for self-confidence, the relationship between the emotional and personal in the learning process, the politics of knowledge, competition among students: these are the themes that resonate throughout this chapter. The contributors here are all both students and teachers, and their writings record their feelings—surprise, doubt, self-confidence, hesitancy, and resistance—toward practicing the feminist values they embrace. They are aware of critical perspectives on concepts such as internalized oppression, the double standard, feminist pedagogy, and the institutional role of feminist scholars, and are struggling to formulate their own perspectives amid these ideas. In short, these contributors share in asking two implicit questions: What kind of teaching do I want? What kind of teacher do I want to be?

The answers that the contributors find to these questions reveal what we call "unarticulated practices" in a feminist education. Unarticulated practices were spawned by the historic exclusion of women from higher education and nurtured by feminist perspectives on hierarchical power structures. They are experienced as alienation from traditional models of teaching and learning. The grounds for these practices lie between an individual's feminist perspective and her (or his) activity within an institutional framework that is based on women's exclusion.

As graduate students who have spent many years in the classroom as students, these contributors confront this territory without formal prepa-

111

ration or support. Indeed, they record resistance from the students they teach as well as resistance from the faculty who employ them to teach. Yet confront it they do, each time they plan a class or interact with those faculty or students—and they have specific ideas about how to proceed. They have taught themselves how to negotiate the distance between their feminist values and the institution in which they work. They have taught themselves to be both self-determined and committed to a community of purpose.

One returning student, Mary-Mallette Acker, confronts her hidden assumption that as a woman she was incapable of creating knowledge. Another contributor, Miriam Peskowitz, wishfully imagines what would happen if "we all just began to pretend that the university was indeed feminist and started acting incredibly surprised when people acted in sexist ways." Charles Paine explores his acceptance of the notion that the personal and political are linked for women, his growing acknowledgment that for him "the personal is problematic" in classroom discussions, and the resulting split between his intellectual and emotional responses. Katie Kent, who has three contributions in this section, reveals that she often must try to help students taking her course who remember or finally acknowledge sexual assault or abuse. She describes how she copes with these emotional realities of women's studies teaching in practical, theoretical, and institutional terms. Martine DeVos decides that she must implement her feminist commitment not only in terms of how she assesses the students' abilities but also in terms of how she assesses her own. Andrea E. maintains that she must keep reminding herself "to pay attention to those voices that seem discordant" with her own, because in academe you are not supposed to admit that you may not know all there is to know. The practices that emerge amid these self-reflections reveal a struggle to reformulate the classroom politics of traditional teacher-student relations. Such reformulations are premised on a commitment to connecting theory with practice, but they are also a matter of necessity.

We trust that this collection of writings opens discussion about learning and teaching practices that emerge from a feminist education. We have identified only a few suggestive categories: empowering oneself to be a creator of knowledge and a visionary, recognizing productive tensions between intellectual and emotional responses, coping with the emotional realities of life, disassembling barriers between teachers and students, and attending to, rather than suppressing, differences of opinion. The unarticulated practices revealed here suggest that the classroom itself may offer a rich beginning point for generating knowledge about the human relationships involved in learning and teaching—with all the myriad complications that that provokes for redefining the relationship between teachers and students. The contributions to this book suggest the promise of the challenge.

MY OWN ABILITY TO LEARN

Mary-Mallette Acker

I was excited this week to have the opportunity to read one single book from cover to cover. I expected to acquire a better handle on what I was reading as a result of having the entire book available to me. I've come to realize that this way of thinking is not entirely valid. Although it is nice to read an entire book as opposed to a chapter or excerpt, it's not the only way to learn or necessarily the most effective way to learn. This may not seem like a revelation to some, but I feel that I have gained a certain amount of confidence in myself and a new understanding of how I approach learning. Basically the one thing that has changed as a result of this new awareness is my appreciation and acceptance of my own ability to learn. Previously I may have been insecure about reading excerpts and doubted my ability to connect with what the author was trying to say. I felt a need to get all the information possible before I would be comfortable forming an opinion or critiquing a certain stance. I'm not suggesting that I don't need to be thorough, but I am recognizing that my personal knowledge gained from life experiences forms a solid base for learning. I guess I believed in a corner of my mind what patriarchy has been reinforcing for years—as a woman, I wasn't capable of creating knowledge, I could only learn and reiterate what I had been taught. I find this leap in awareness remarkable.

WHAT IF WE STOPPED RECOGNIZING THEIR AUTHORITY?

Miriam Peskowitz

Funny how we in women's studies are so concerned with the issue of the relationship between the emotional/personal and the scholarly. Yet, a male professor I've had thinks nothing of spending ten to fifteen minutes each class telling personal anecdotes, or of writing his personal piques (even using first-person language!) in articles which he publishes in "respectable" journals. In his case, the connection seems charming, affording a more intimate view of a formidable scholar. I wonder if my reaction would differ if a female professor acted similarly. The case of females being "personal" in the classroom brings an entirely different set of reactions for me. So that this one action, done by professors of different genders, produces different reactions. What if we all just began to pretend that the university was indeed feminist, and started acting incredibly surprised when people acted in sexist ways; what if we made marginal the people who try to marginalize those of us who are feminist? What if we stopped recognizing their authority?

This, of course, doesn't change the structure of the institution or the attitudes which others hold; I certainly don't believe that thinking something is changed actually changes it. But when I stopped seeing myself and my ideas as marginal, I gained some confidence, stopped apologizing for feminist ideas, and felt stronger and more comfortable articulating my views to people who didn't necessarily share them.

ACKNOWLEDGING EMOTION

Katie Kent

For some women's studies teachers, to acknowledge or validate emotion is to enforce the stereotype of women's studies, that is that it is just a bunch of women sitting around experiencing themselves and talking about how things make them feel. I must admit I have a hard time when that kind of stuff starts happening in my classes. Part of that has to do with my internalization of exactly the same fears these women expressed—that perhaps women's studies *isn't* valid when it starts to privilege feelings and experience. On the other hand, experience, the unique and *different* experiences of women, is what founded and maintains women's studies. But it's incredibly hard to achieve a balance between excessive emoting and excessive academicizing, at least for me it is, both in my own life as well as in my classes. I can't even imagine what would happen if I were trying to reach and change men who have never been taught how to even begin to deal with the emotional realities uncovered by feminist work. In class when things get out of hand, when someone really becomes inappropriate, I usually try to maneuver her/him into talking to me individually, and then suggest appropriate ways of handling whatever issues have been raised for the student (which usually means a referral and perhaps a list of readings). For example, I often have students remember or finally acknowledge sexual assault or abuse which they had either suppressed or had never been allowed to think of as rape before. This is a crucial moment, one that illustrates both the importance and power of women's studies.

THE PERSONAL IS PROBLEMATIC

Charles Paine

Humanists are now under siege because they say the humanities make students into better, more free-thinking human beings, but they don't say how; it simply magically happens somehow—a leap of faith. I'm sometimes afraid that the connection between personal action and political action requires the same sort of faithful leap. I understand the theories of collective action and radical pedagogy, but still, I find myself distrusting it somewhat, perhaps because of my own doubts about my personal capacities.

Obviously, then, making the transition from the personal to the political is especially problematic for me, since I tend to distrust anything personal. When in class we'd discuss personal experiences, I often found myself asking, "What's the point, where's this leading?" I enjoyed it and found it stimulating, but I was worried—worried perhaps that what we were doing wasn't *serious* enough, that it was only "shop talk." My motto might be, "The personal is problematic." Emotionally I continue to distrust ideas that are based on personal experience; I suppose I don't consider them "objective" enough, even though I understand (perhaps too fully) the problems of calling anything "objective." But intellectually, I've been swayed to concluding that all politics come from personal grounding, and I have to learn to trust myself enough that I can proceed from there.

IS TEACHING WOMEN'S STUDIES INHERENTLY POLITICAL?

Katie Kent

Is teaching women's studies or feminist theory inherently political? Is it a political act with specific consequences? I suppose I would answer yes, but . . . (as I do many other questions associated with feminist theory). Yes, but what does it mean to teach young coeds about sex-role stereotypes and women's history and feminist revisions of the canon? Does it make them any more sensitive to the women who scrub the floors of their dormitories, or to their own positions in the world outside the university? Maybe I'm just feeling cynical and embittered this evening. I know from my own experience of TA'ing women's studies courses that, unlike any others, I see concrete changes and both intellectual and emotional responses in my students. I see them wrestle with various issues that pertain to their personal, economic, political, and academic lives. I see it as one of the only places in the university where what I say and what I teach makes an actual *difference* in some of my students' lives. And by the mere fact that I am teaching at all, I feel as though I am making a dent in the power structure that has for so long silenced and ignored the contributions and realities of women. When I lead a class on sexuality or class or race I know even the words I am speaking are politically charged, words like "lesbian" and "working-class."

Yet I also see women and men adapting the tools of feminist theory without any apparent self-examination or political commitment. As an academic tool, as these authors so aptly portray, feminist theory can illuminate and redefine almost every area of scholarship. Thus, perhaps it is not surprising that one can make a statement such as "I am really interested in the ways feminist modes of inquiry apply to my work in X, but I don't believe in its political tenets at all." Perhaps this (what I consider) false (and maybe even violent) sense of the separation of theory and practice is in part produced by the severing of feminist theory from its interdisciplinary underpinnings or anchor. Taking one bit of theory while leaving its practical implications behind is easier, it seems to me, when one ignores the multifaceted origins and debates that produce and enliven feminist thinking.

EASIER SAID THAN DONE

Martine DeVos

Obviously, I believe that if one calls oneself a feminist, one should attempt to put those beliefs into practice. As a teacher (or as a person generally), that's easier said than done. Almost automatically, I tend to think more highly of students who participate in class and less of students who never say a thing. Almost automatically, I tend to forget about the "quiet ones" once I'm on a roll in the classroom. The latter, of course, can be remedied by being more conscious of involving those students *or* by shutting up altogether and letting the students run the class (which, often, is accompanied by a feeling that I'm not doing my job). The former, the attaching of higher value to (mildly) aggressive behavior, is more deeply ingrained and more difficult to remedy. In a course where you cannot assign exact numbers to a student's performance and in which they are not tested on "facts," grades are almost necessarily subjective. How does one set the standard if one wants to incorporate feminist beliefs in one's practice? Doing away with grades would be an obvious solution, but we can't, given this institution in which we are working. Giving everyone an "A" also doesn't work for me, because I want to reward those who work very hard. Although I grapple with this problem every semester, I can't say I've found a solution.

Encouraging female students, talking about sexism in the ways it affects our lives, is a bit easier, and something I take much pleasure in. Again, I constantly have to fight the feeling that—when we're discussing sexism in society and giving examples from personal lives—I'm not doing my job, that we're just "shooting the shit." Although I'm aware that this feeling is unjust, it's nonetheless persistent *despite* (or perhaps *because* of) the fact that my students always engage more actively in discussion, that they seem to *enjoy* these discussions most, and that they seem to *remember* them most as well. I guess part of me continues to carry around an internalized idea that this stuff is not serious, not Knowledge, and that learning shouldn't really be fun when you get down to it. That doesn't mean you give up on trying to continue to do these things in the classroom; it means that it's difficult work.

FEMINIST PEDAGOGY AND AUTHORITY

Elana Newman

I have been advising a student for almost a year and a half on an independent study project. In my department the faculty is often so overloaded that students seldom get access to faculty members, so we have arranged it so that I advise a handful of students under my faculty advisor's independent study status; in exchange the students do some sort of work that will assist my research, and help them understand research, thinking, etc. It has been a wonderful enterprise, and over the years with one student I have felt that we have collaborated well. I feel that I have been able to help her develop intellectually in terms of the process of thinking.

We have discussed the work in terms of culture, the university structure, the psychological state, and have been able to engage in fruitful thought exercises. Personally it has helped me get a better sense of some small proportion of students. The structure itself has been feminist, in that the work extends to the personal implications. Throughout the last year and a half, we have worked effectively within a three-party hierarchical structure and negotiated the problems it posed, but we had never discussed the nature of the structure and power lines between us. Yesterday I suggested for closure that we move away from the project and do some work on looking at the structure and movement of the work in terms of authority lines as well as intellectual lines. It has been exciting to work with an individual student, to be able to give the resources I have, admit those I don't, and create an educational forum together in a structure and negotiate a useful enterprise.

My formal TA work has been more cumbersome in dealing with authority issues and structure, and I have not yet figured out how to integrate feminist pedagogy successfully in that format. I certainly need to improve my factual knowledge and ability to lecture. In my work as a TA in teaching sections, I have tried not to be an authority, to foster a community of learning, and there the structure seems very different. I am deemed an expert, and the students have expected me to take the responsibility all the time for discussion. Actually as it has evolved one of my classes is extremely successful and the other is terrible. It is difficult to assess the best ways to teach students at different stages of intellectual development, with different ideas about the classroom, and with varying degrees of authority and motivation to encounter the material. It is a continual struggle to evaluate the work of these endeavors.

KNOWING ALL THERE IS TO KNOW

Andrea E.

The performance aspect in most classrooms has bothered me a great deal of late; I don't understand what happened to the idea that we are all here to learn. Now it seems everyone has to prove what he or she already knows. . . . I think this expresses, in part, the kind of anxiety I've experienced in the classroom (being well-read, being politically correct, proving yourself constantly). I have an impulse to treat my journal writing as if it was a place where all the contradictions and inconsistencies are supposed to be worked out to create a smooth and professional product. Of course that means that perceived contradictions in one's work must also get "smoothed over" "for the sake of argument." I have found this "professional"/"scholarly" practice to be misleading in so many ways, not the least of which is making me block out those things that perhaps would prove most interesting to follow through—those points where everything isn't really fitting together as it should, and which I cannot acknowledge because I have such a stake in proving myself through this argument I've been following. I have tried to change this way of writing papers, doing research, but it's an ongoing project. I have to keep reminding myself to pay attention to those voices that seem discordant with my own. And I think this type of behavior is something I have had to learn to survive so far in academe—where more often I have been made to feel ashamed for not getting something "right" or for simply not knowing what "of course" I should have known, than encouraged to speak in an environment fostering mutual discovery. The rare instances when I have come across such situations have been when the balance of power, the professor's "authority" has been displaced—something that happens mostly in women's studies courses and sometimes when the professor does not have a territorial relationship to his/her subject matter. It's difficult to admit that you may not know all there is to know about something, especially when you will be held accountable by the institution that employs you. But I think the facade of knowing all there is to know, the figure of inviolable authority "the professor" usually assumes is a deeply misguided one. It's up there with the idea that there should be a literary canon, that there are a group of texts which are "classics." Knowledge is not value and context free— and it's often more interesting to examine what someone knows and the gaps in that knowledge as reflective of a cultural, sociopolitical, institutional, temporal phenomenon (among other factors) than to make her (or him) feel inadequate in a particular realm by holding her accountable for a predetermined set of discourses.

FEMINISM WAS A DIRTY WORD

Martine DeVos

In every course I have taught so far, I have attempted to integrate questions of gender. In every course, and especially in freshman courses, I have encountered strong resistance from the students, all of whom perceive *feminism* as a very dirty word—a word that conjures up images of bra-burning, man-hating, possibly homosexual, women. Inevitably, in every course so far I've tossed the syllabus at a certain point and addressed the "dirtiness" of the F-word. This semester, in part because of my fuller understanding of feminist history, I must say the Day of Reckoning went a lot better. I also discovered that, in part, it went better because I personalized the question. That is, I told personal anecdotes: how I thought *feminism* was a dirty word when I was a freshman, how my realization of sexism in the world around me included some painful realizations about my friends/family/myself, etc. The students were unusually responsive this time, and I think in part it was the result of bringing the debate down to the "real world" (as they call it) level—a level to which they can relate and a level that makes students understand how and why a certain person might become a feminist without having been born that way, or without having had "bad experiences" with men, etc.

Which brings me to a second lesson. I think it's important for all feminists, including those who teach or are involved in curriculum integration projects, to refrain from a holier-than-thou attitude. I think it's easy to fall into, and I also think it repulses those who might be more sympathetic otherwise. An attitude of "we're all in this together, patriarchy stinks, but it's not only men who buy into it" is, I think, ultimately more productive. In part, because it is more realistic. I think all of us who are sympathetic to or call ourselves partners in the feminist cause are not above falling into certain sexist behavior or thought patterns once in a while. That recognition is important, not only because it forces one to think about one's own behavior and the extensive nature of patriarchy, but also because it might soften one's attitude and/or approach toward those who are at a less advanced (if I may use this term) stage of recognizing sexism in society.

THE DOMINANT RECIPE FOR KNOWLEDGE

Catherine B. Kleiner

My feeling is that women's studies cannot remain a separate discipline forever, if it wants to truly transform the academy. Only enlightened people (who we know are the minority in this world) will pursue women's studies—the hoards of unenlightened will remain untouched by its influences. Yet at the same time, many women trained in women's studies will function as scholars in specific disciplines, reaching students who can ultimately become enlightened by example.

I have difficulty seeing feminist research bringing about complete revolutionary change or a *gestalt* switch where old and new theories are inadequate. I see feminist research as contributory or additive to existing theoretical frameworks. Feminist theory and feminist research cannot possibly completely replace what exists already. It can point to flaws in existing theories and act as a corrective force, but feminist research and method cannot stand alone. It is a necessary and until recently undervalued ingredient in the dominant recipe for knowledge, but it cannot be seen as a separate "paradigm" that will completely replace what history has provided us. Perhaps I am a conservative in that sense, or maybe more evolutionary than revolutionary in my views regarding the impact and use of feminist research in the academy. All feminists in the academy must first be revisionists—they must be sure that women's perspectives and experiences are always included, but feminists themselves must never be exclusionary.

THE POWER OF INTERDISCIPLINARY PERSPECTIVES

Katie Kent

While, as in feminist politics, the eventual goal of women's studies would logically be its own demise (and this is my own standpoint on the issue), it could only end as a distinct discipline when women succeed in ending their own oppression (with the help of others of course). So, there is a need for both an autonomous women's studies program, and simultaneously there is a need to integrate it into all the disciplines. But what about the women who are coming up in the ranks, the students who want to get Ph.D.'s in women's studies, the many universities which may be on the verge of making that important leap from the title "women's studies program" to "women's studies department," something which implies a whole new level of legitimacy, since a department by definition implies disciplinary boundaries and methodologies, not to mention institutional legitimacy and full-time paid faculty members? But how many courses in "women's studies" should a student take? Shouldn't they also take courses in a variety of disciplines that explore a multiplicity of ways of analyzing the roles and oppressions of women? Again we come back to the point or characteristic of women's studies that is both its strength and its source of controversy, namely that its power comes from its many interdisciplinary perspectives. The fact that these perspectives are often in conflict, I would argue, as I did above, makes it even more powerful as it places much responsibility on individual students and/or scholars to make their own decisions as to which methodologies and ideological tenets they believe are the ones most satisfactory for their goals, beliefs, and selves.

BEING A TEACHER

Kathryn West

How do I want to define myself as a member of this profession? I know we get jobs, tenure, and promotions on the basis of publications, but teaching is a really important aspect of it all for me. When I decided to go to graduate school, it was probably the thing I felt most unsure about—I've always been fairly quiet and reserved, and wasn't sure how well I'd be able to get up in front of a class and talk. Now, it is one of the things I like best. And, of course, along the way I discovered that the better modes of teaching (at least those that are better in my view) do not revolve around standing in front of a class and pontificating, but rather concentrate on setting up an environment in which people can talk, discuss, explore, agree, disagree, and expand their visions. Lecturing has a place in my classes, but not the primary place. And it's so exhilarating when conversations do start happening. I know I still have a lot to learn about being a teacher, but it's heartening to look back over the past three years and see how I've grown—both as a teacher and because of being one.

NINE

The Politics of Knowledge: Taking Action

Studies about the impact of women's studies on students attempt to answer, with aggregate data, questions such as, Are students' attitudes toward themselves, toward women, changed by women's studies classes? Do they graduate from college better prepared for life in the modern world? Are they more conscious of discrimination against women in general, and can they effectively fight it when it is directed at them, in particular? [1] By and large, the answer to all of the above is "yes."

Less is known about the impact of women's studies students on their institutions. If, indeed, women students are routinely silenced and marginalized in the classroom, then it would seem that those whose course of study prepares them for this experience will be stronger than most— more prepared and more willing to confront a professor about casual sexist remarks, to speak out about sexual harassment and the campus climate for women, to commit their intellectual and personal lives to creating an environment that is a constructive and nurturing learning experience for women. We know from the contributors in *Engaging Feminism*, however, that these actions are not taken without self-doubt, even in the steadiest heart. To take action is, in effect, to change the rules, to challenge the notion that the rules are unchangeable, to challenge what is accepted as the "truth," the "way things are," "reality." One of the most important contributions of women's studies may be its ability to expose these concepts as value-laden collaborators in systems of political power.

Throughout this collection there are instances of students naming the rules of behavior and performance to which they are expected to comply. In this chapter, we present three long documents that were created by students as a part of the process of envisioning a woman-friendly academy. Each document represents a history of grievances that the students want to voice and begin addressing. The first, " 'Sir'vey or 'Madam'vey," is a 1989 seminar paper that resulted from feminist graduate students' systematic attempts to collect information about the problems they experienced in their botany and zoology departments the previous year. The authors created the questionnaire, collected and compiled the data, and wrote the paper within the context of their training as scientists, their commitment to empirical data, and their critique of the gender politics of their departments. They presented their research results at a seminar jointly sponsored by the two departments. More than fifty students attended; only a few faculty came. They sent copies of the seminar paper and survey results to the faculty and graduate students in botany and zoology, and to the dean of the graduate school, who forwarded copies to the university's president, provost, and dean of the school of arts and sciences. The immediate effect of these efforts was small. There was little change in departmental dynamics, and after supportive comments from the administration, the initiative seemed to fade. Yet, in the two years since the survey was conducted and the paper written, the small changes have had a cumulative effect. Searches for new faculty have been more inclusive of women, and four graduate students (including two of the authors) participated with faculty in a discussion group on women and science issues which has helped to lay the groundwork for a university-wide project to educate science faculty about gender issues. One of the authors has been hired to team-teach a women's studies seminar on the feminist critique of science. Another set of students have proposed a lecture series featuring women scientists that has been endorsed by their department. All of these developments followed from the initial insight that there was a need to research and document the differences between women's and men's experience in graduate school.

The second document is an account of efforts to effect institutional change once the need for change had become apparent. A small group of graduate students worked collectively to articulate their concerns, call them to the attention of department administrators, and outline strategies that would promote change. The students engaged in these activities had not initiated them as classroom exercises—they were putting themselves at risk, politically, within their institutional framework in order to improve the climate in which they sought an education. They were willing to take the risk because they had become immobilized by the tensions between their commitment to their professional training and their critique of the gender politics of that training. In their view, the time had come to initiate productive change.

The authors of "Systems and Actions: Reflecting on Change" have omitted the name of the department from their documents and the account of the events that transpired. Their analysis began in specific, personal experiences when one student decided to drop out of graduate school. As she reconsidered her decision, she came to see that the problems she confronted were part of a larger pattern in the department's gender dynamics. Having decided to return to graduate school, and in concert with a community of women in the graduate program, she wrote the memo that began a series of exchanges with various committees and administrators within the department in order to explain some of the problems they encountered and to propose remedies for them. It is unusual to have a series of letters and memos, with reports of responses to them, that spell out the perspectives and approaches of the various actors. The events documented, along with the authors' retrospective on them, testify both to the depths of the problems and the resistance of the structures to addressing them.

Like the initiatives of the botany and zoology students, in the short term this exchange of memos seemed to have accomplished little. Yet, two years later, feminist scholarship has a more secure place in the department's graduate program. A feminist scholar has assumed the position of director of graduate studies and has had a noticeable impact on decisions about graduate funding. The attention and discussion that gender issues received in this department in the last two years has resulted in a significant increase in the percentage of its majors taking women's studies classes. Again, the energy and persistence of these women initiated a process of departmental self-reflection that continues to promote change.

The final document takes this process of naming the problems, and then initiating institutional change, one step further by recounting the story of a feminist reading group—that is, a group of women who decided to create a positive learning environment for themselves. It is not unusual for groups of graduate students to meet together for a common purpose. The students behind "Systems and Actions" first met for social purposes and then evolved into an action-oriented group. Graduate students set up study groups for prelims, or they meet over a particular theoretical issue.

Some students create dissertation writing groups to support one another throughout the lonely and exacting process of completing their doctorates. What is unusual about the group who wrote "The Evolution and Process of a Successful Graduate Feminist Reading Group" is the diversity of backgrounds and interests of the participants, the length of time that it sustained itself, and the degree to which they were willing to examine what bound them together. As their tale makes clear, that process of self-examination itself became the vehicle for their successes. They met their need for a home, for a safe place within the academy, only to discover that together they shared a greater commitment: "We want to make a difference in people's lives, beginning with our own."

1. Christine Bose, John Steiger, and Philomina Victorine, "Evaluation: Perspectives of Students and Graduates," *Women's Studies Newsletter* 5, no. 4 (Fall 1977): 6–7; Lorelei R. Brush, Alice Ross Gold, and Marni Goldstein White, "The Paradox of Intention and Effect: A Women's Studies Course," *Signs* 3, no. 4 (Summer 1978): 870–83. For a divergent view, see Nancy M. Porter and Margaret T. Eileenchild, *The Effectiveness of Women's Studies Teaching* (Washington, D.C.: U.S. Government Printing Office, 1980).

"SIR"VEY OR "MADAM"VEY?

Banu Subramaniam, Rebecca Dunn, and Lynn E. Broaddus

The following seminar paper was delivered to the Departments of Botany and Zoology on October 20, 1989.

This survey comes as a response to a discussion group on gender and science which students from Botany and Zoology organized in summer 1989. A number of issues were raised that concerned various aspects of graduate student life and many appeared to be gender specific. In order to address some of these problems, we decided to poll graduate students in our departments as a way of answering some of the questions we had. The questionnaire that we wrote was distributed to all graduate students in the Departments of Botany and Zoology who are in residence at the main campus. Our intent was simply to investigate the patterns of thought among our peers, and to see how those thoughts varied according to gender and academic age. It is our hope that these results will help us all see academia through each other's eyes and will let people know that they are not alone in their uncertainties or self-doubts.

Before presenting the results of our survey, we would like to present a framework by briefly describing the results of other studies. We shall first consider some professional indicators of the relative success of men and women in academia. The gaps between the two sexes have narrowed substantially over the past decade, but according to published reports, significant differences still remain. A 1973 study (Bayer and Astin, 1975) showed that even after experience level and publication record were accounted for, women academics were still paid less than men. According to 1987 data from the National Research Council, women Ph.D. biologists earn only 85 percent of what men earn, and this difference holds up across all experience categories (Vetter, 1989). A 1988 survey of the members of the Ecological Society of America showed that in every age category women's salaries averaged less than men's (Travis, 1989).

If one measures productivity by publication record, it seems that men publish more frequently than women. This is often frustrating because

A coin toss decided that the authors' names should appear in reverse alphabetical order. We want to emphasize the equal participation, equal work, and equal glory.

there have been very few studies on the nature of the different publication patterns. In one of these few studies, Primack and O'Leary (1989) examined the publication records of past students from the Organization for Tropical Studies and found that, after accounting for academic age, men published more than women. A closer look, however, showed that for the most part men and women had identical publication records, but that 10 percent of the men were super-productive and raised the overall mean for their gender. Of significance is that none of the women surveyed fell into this superachiever category.

Another study (Sih and Nishikawa, 1988) tested the hypothesis that men and women publish different types of work, specifically that they have unequal rates of publishing notes and comments. In the three journals investigated, *Evolution, American Naturalist*, and *Science*, male authors of letters and comments outnumbered female authors by 14:1, 18:1, and 7:1 respectively. These proportions far outweighed the sex ratio in the journals' full-length articles and support the hypothesis that some of the difference between men's and women's publication records is due to the nature of the publications rather than the research productivity of the scientists.

Another factor which has been thought to affect publication rates is that women have traditionally borne more of the responsibilities of marriage and child rearing. Cole and Zuckerman's 1987 study indicates, however, that married women with and without children and single women have equal publication records.

Is it possible that women postpone publication until they are extremely confident of their results? The answer is unclear, but it has been shown that men and women differ significantly in their confidence in themselves and their work. For example, in one study (cited in Widnall, 1988), a group of high school valedictorians was surveyed over several years to find out how they ranked themselves over time. At the time of graduation equal proportions of boys and girls considered themselves average, above average, etc. But by the time of college graduation none of the women continued to view themselves as far above average, whereas one-quarter of the men still had superior opinions of themselves.

In extensive polls taken of the graduate students at Stanford and MIT (Widnall, 1988), it was found that men and women had very similar career goals, equal preparedness in graduate school, and equal performance while in graduate school. Despite this apparent equality, women were more likely to seriously consider dropping out of graduate school and had much lower confidence in their ability to succeed in their field.

Most probably part of this difference is due to different ways men and women internalize their experiences, but it may also be due to the subtle differences in the way men and women are treated. For instance, at MIT and Stanford it was shown that women are less likely to be supported on a research assistantship, thus cutting them off from one important source of student-advisor interaction as well as making it more difficult for them to obtain research time (Widnall, 1988).

Women meet with their advisors less often, have fewer major responsibilities in their research groups, are interrupted more frequently than men, receive less eye contact in classroom situations, and are more reluctant to take credit for their own accomplishments. Women graduate students are more likely to receive no financial support. In addition, in a world where most advisors are men, women are less apt to engage in after-hour socializing with their advisors.

The subtle discrimination often continues after graduate school as well. In studies of invited speakers at the Ecological Society of America's meetings in recent years, it was found that when the inviting panel included women, women were invited to speak in proportion with their representation in the field. But when the inviters were all men, women were invited to speak at one-third that rate (Gurevitch, 1988).

These differences in the way men and women experience academia have a significant effect on our ability to recruit women into science teaching and research. A recent study by the Office of Technology Assessment (Widnall, 1988) showed that of two thousand girls and two thousand boys in the ninth grade, only half of each group will have enough math and science skills to remain in the math/science "pipeline." As their education proceeds, fewer and fewer will have enough background to remain in the pipeline, but by the end of graduate level education far fewer women than men will remain. This is despite the fact that women enter graduate school, including prestigious programs, in the same proportion as men. The times when women drop out of the pipeline at a rate much higher than men are between high school graduation and choice of career in college, and during graduate school. This means that women must be dropping out, or stopping at master's degrees more frequently than men, and the reasons for this must be tied into the graduate school experience, which brings us to the results of our survey.

The graduate students of the Botany and Zoology Departments were surveyed about their perceptions and attitudes toward graduate school to determine whether this gender effect that has been established on a

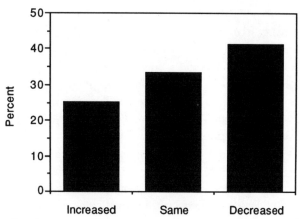

FIG. 1: How has your self-confidence changed since you entered graduate school?

national level also exists at Duke. There was excellent participation in the survey. Seventy-two percent of the graduate students (75 out of 104) returned the surveys, including 35 women and 40 men. Of those 75, 33 have taken their preliminary exams. To ascertain whether gender was confounded by the qualifications of students, the GRE's and GPA's of women and men admitted to the Departments of Botany and Zoology between 1983 and 1985 were compared. It was determined that there was no difference between the two sexes; in fact, if anything female students were better qualified. After it was established that women and men do not differ in their capabilities when entering graduate school, the data was analyzed using Analysis of Variance from SAS (SAS Institute, Inc.) with gender, age in graduate school, and prelim completion as the independent variables. This survey explores the graduate experiences of both sexes.

The first question examined how graduate school has affected self-confidence. Of all the students who were surveyed, 41 percent felt that their experiences in graduate school caused a decrease in self-confidence and only 26 percent felt an increase in self-confidence (see fig. 1). There was a significant gender effect [p = 0.05] with women experiencing a greater loss of self-confidence. Over 50 percent of the women suffered a decrease in confidence whereas only 33 percent of the men felt a loss of confidence (see fig. 2). To examine the issue of self-esteem more closely, students were asked to rank their intellectual abilities relative to their peers. There was again a significant gender effect [p = 0.037] with women consistently ranking themselves lower than men (see fig. 3). Remember, women and men start graduate school with equal qualifications. A similar

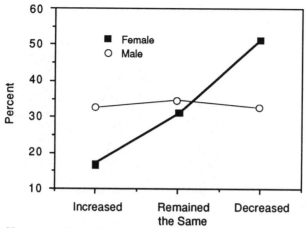

FIG. 2: Has your self-confidence changed since you entered graduate school?

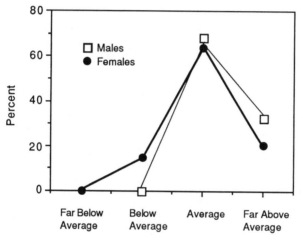

FIG. 3: How do you rank your intellectual abilities relative to your peers at Duke?

trend [p = 0.06] was found when women and men were asked how their peers would rank them relative to others. Women tended to think their peers would rank them lower than did men, but it was not significant. This pattern has been found before in other studies and has been termed the "imposter syndrome," which refers to the theory that some women rank themselves lower than they think their peers would and have the accompanying fear of eventually being "found out" (Widnall, 1988).

The next series of questions investigated the students' intentions of quitting and their reasons. Of all the students surveyed, 70 percent had

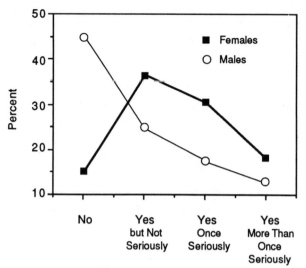

FIG. 4: Have you ever considered quitting graduate school?

considered quitting graduate school. Here again there is a significant gender effect [p = 0.028], as figure 4 shows that 85 percent of the women considered quitting compared to 55 percent of the men. Furthermore, women consistently chose each category (i.e., yes but not seriously, yes once seriously, yes more than once seriously) more frequently than men. The reasons for quitting, however, show no gender differences, but it is striking that 37 percent of the students thought of leaving graduate school because they disliked the academic environment and work expectations; 25 percent cited personal inadequacy; 13 percent thought graduate school too demanding of one's time; and only 11 percent quit for monetary reasons. Another important result was the interaction between quitting and self-evaluation [p = 0.0015] (see fig. 5), which shows that all those who ranked themselves below average had thought about quitting whereas 45 percent of those who ranked themselves above average had never considered it. The interaction between self-confidence and quitting shows the same pattern and is also significant [p = 0.016].

Since survey results show that many students are dissatisfied with the academic environment, it is of interest to see what career choices students are considering. The results were as follows: 24 percent chose a large research-oriented university; 36 percent a small teaching-oriented college; 17 percent a private nonprofit organization; 4 percent science writing; 4 percent industry; 7 percent other science-related jobs; and 7 percent nonscience jobs. It is interesting that 40 percent of the students

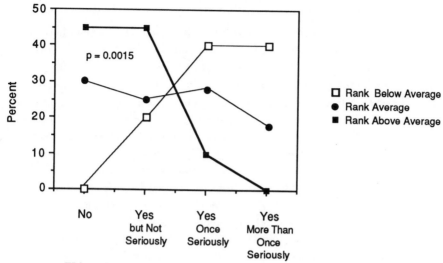

FIG. 5: Interaction between quitting and self-evaluation.

do not want to become faculty and less than a quarter wish to go to a university like Duke. It is also noteworthy that no gender effects exist. It should be stressed that there were also no gender effects in the number of hours female and male students would be happy to work and expected to work in the job of their choice. Needless to say, at whatever job they chose, people expected to work more hours than they would like!

The next set of questions examines how students perceive their strengths and weaknesses. There were ten choices: experimental design, asking big questions, teaching, statistics, technical innovation, organization, self-discipline, writing, speaking, and administration. Significant gender effects were found for (1) statistics [$p = 0.0167$]—15 percent of the men considered statistics a strength, but none of the women found it to be a strength; (2) organization [$p = 0.05$]—61 percent of the women vs. 40 percent of the men decided organization was a strength; (3) asking big questions [$p = 0.0027$]—significantly more women found this to be a weakness. To summarize the trends, we divided the abilities into two categories: (1) teaching and administrative strengths (teaching organization, self-discipline, administration) and (2) academic research skills (experimental design, asking big questions, statistics, and technical innovations). Teaching and administrative strengths showed a significant gender effect [$p = 0.05$] with women perceiving these qualities as strengths. Conversely, women thought of academic and research qualities as weaknesses [$p = 0.02$].

When asked to what they attributed their success, women chose categories that are considered external to self (i.e., luck, simplicity of the task, hard work, and help of others) while men chose innate ability, which is considered to be internal and is an integral part of one's self-esteem. However, when each category was examined for gender effects, only one was found to be significant. Women felt that the main reason for their success was the simplicity of the task. Women picked this category significantly more often than men [p = 0.038]. Interestingly, there was a very significant effect with age and innate ability [p = 0.0027]; 82 percent of the students who had not taken their preliminary exams said their innate abilities were a reason for their success, but only 12 percent of those who had taken their prelims felt that their success was due to their innate ability.

Finally, in response to the question of whether students had felt discriminated against (subtly or overtly) during their time at Duke, there was a significant gender effect [p = 0.0002] with 44 percent of the women feeling discrimination vs. 7 percent of the men. This result falls in the range of the national average.

In conclusion, graduate school appears to be a very trying and difficult experience for all students. However, this survey shows (as others have) that women experience graduate school very differently from their male counterparts. Although women come into school with equal if not better qualifications, the graduate school experience significantly affects their self-esteem and perceptions. To summarize the findings, women consistently rank their intellectual abilities lower than men, experience lowered self-confidence, consider quitting more often (85 percent vs. 55 percent), and perceive academic skills which are central to doing research as weaknesses. Furthermore, when they do succeed, they belittle their success by passing the task off as much too simple. Also, 44 percent of the women feel they have felt discrimination (overtly/subtly) at Duke.

Several factors are probably at work which would result in the above outcome. One reason that is often cited is the lack of female role models. Currently three of the twenty-one faculty members in Zoology are women, and none of the eighteen faculty members in Botany are women. We also investigated the proportion of women from outside the department who were invited to give seminars at three seminar series; i.e., Zoology departmental seminar series (5.6 percent were women), University Program of Genetics seminar series (14 percent were women), and the Plant Ecology seminar series (24 percent were women). Although the goal is to have 50 percent women, the current pool of women in life sciences is only 20 percent. Not only was this figure rather low, but also two of the three seminar series invited women at a disproportionately lower rate than that of their presence in the field.

Several other factors outlined in the introduction presumably contribute to this overall effect. We encourage students in other departments to look into the environment in their own departments. We see this survey as a first step to combatting the rather chilly climate for women in academia. We are at present trying to identify specific issues in the environment and structure of graduate school that adversely affect women. It is our belief that by addressing these issues, we will improve the climate for all graduate students and will be helping women take a step toward achieving their rightful place in academia. We would like to leave you with the words of Maria Mitchell, a woman astronomer, who had this to say over a century ago: "In my younger days, when I was pained by the half-educated, loose and inaccurate ways which we [women] all had, I used to say, 'How much women need exact science,' but since I have known some workers in science who were not always true to the teachings of nature, who have loved self more than science, I have now said, 'How much science needs women'" (Maria Mitchell's presidential address to the Third Congress of Women in 1875; quoted in Rossiter, 1982, p. 15).

Acknowledgments: We would like to thank Dr. Lucinda McDade for her encouragement and support, Dr. Diana Freckman for her interest and help, Peggy Schultz, Meg Ronsheim, and Chantal Reid for their editing and continuing enthusiasm, and all the graduate students in Botany and Zoology for their excellent participation.

Literature Cited

BAYER, ALAN E., AND HELEN S. ASTIN. 1975. Sex differentials in the academic reward system. *Science* 188: 796–802.

COLE, JONATHAN R., AND HARRIET ZUCKERMAN. 1987. Marriage, motherhood, and research performance in science. *Scientific American* 256 (2): 119–25.

GUREVITCH, JESSICA. 1988. Differences in the proportion of women to men invited to give seminars: Is the old boy still kicking? *Bulletin of the Ecological Society of America* (hereafter *BESA*) 69: 155–60.

PRIMACK, RICHARD B., AND VIRGINIA O'LEARY. 1989. Research productivity of men and women ecologists: A longitudinal study of former graduate students. *BESA* 70: 7–12.

ROSSITER, M. W. 1982. *Women scientists in America: Struggles & strategies in 1940*. Baltimore: Johns Hopkins University Press.

SIH, ANDREW, AND KIISA NISHIKAWA. 1988. Do men and women really differ in publication rates and contentiousness? An empirical survey. *BESA* 69: 15–18.

TRAVIS, JOSEPH. 1989. Results of the survey of the membership of the Ecological Society of America: 1987–1988. *BESA* 70: 78–88.

VETTER, BETTY M. 1989. Bad news for women scientists—and the country. *AAAS Observer*, 5 May 1989, p. 10.

WIDNALL, SHEILA E. 1988. AAAS Presidential Lecture: Voices from the pipeline. *Science* 241: 1740–45.

Appendix 1
Bozo Survey

Please answer these questions honestly. All surveys are completely anonymous. Survey results will be shared with all Botany and Zoology graduate students as soon as they have been tallied.

When you complete your survey, please put it into the envelope on the front desk.

1. This will be my _____ year in graduate school.
   a. first or second   b. third or fourth   c. fifth or greater

2. Have you taken your preliminary examination yet? (Answer "yes" even if you have taken it but not yet passed.)
   a. yes   b. no

3. What is your sex?
   a. male   b. female

4. How do you rank your intellectual abilities relative to your peers at Duke?
   a. far below average   b. below average   c. average
   d. above average   e. far above average

5. How do you think your peers would rank you relative to others at Duke?
    a. far below average   b. below average   c. average
    d. above average   e. far above average

6. How has your self-confidence changed since you entered graduate school?
    a. increased   b. remained the same   c. decreased

7. At any point in your graduate career, have you considered quitting?
    a. no   b. yes, but not seriously   c. yes, once very seriously
    d. yes, more than once very seriously

8. If you answered "yes" to the above question, what was your primary reason for considering quitting?
    a. monetary
    b. too demanding of one's time
    c. personal inadequacy
    d. dislike of academic environment and work expectations
    e. other_____

9. After graduate school (and postdoctoral positions, if any) what type of career do you currently most desire to have?
    a. faculty position at a large, research-oriented university
    b. faculty position at a smaller, more teaching-oriented school
    c. position at a private, nonprofit organization
    d. science writing
    e. industry
    f. other science-related job_____
    g. nonscience job_____
(Note: For the purposes of this survey, raising your own children shall be considered a nonscience job.)

10. In the job which you envision for yourself, how many hours per week would you
    a. be happy to work_____
    b. expect to have to work_____
   (In your calculation, include work-related hours spent at home.)

11. What do you see as your strengths? (Circle as many or as few as you like.)

        a. experimental design   g. self-discipline
        b. asking "big" questions   h. writing
        c. teaching   i. speaking
        d. statistics   j. administrative
        e. technical innovation   k. other_____
        f. organization

12. What do you see as your weaknesses?

        a. experimental design   g. self-discipline
        b. asking "big" questions   h. writing
        c. teaching   i. speaking
        d. statistics   j. administrative
        e. technical innovation   k. other_____
        f. organization

13. To which of the following are you most likely to attribute your successes?

        a. luck   b. hard work   c. simplicity of the task
        d. your innate ability   e. the help of others

14. Do you feel that at any time during your time at Duke you have been discriminated against (either subtly or overtly) for either your sex or your ethnic/economic status?

        a. no   b. yes

If you would like to elaborate on any of your responses, please feel free to do so.

Thanks.

SYSTEMS AND ACTIONS: REFLECTING ON CHANGE

Cathy S. and Emma C.

In fall of 1989 several women in our graduate department formed a group to act on problems related to gender. In the course of that semester we talked to each other and wrote to our peers, colleagues, and faculty about the unacceptable situation women face in our department. We gathered around kitchen tables laid with chips, popcorn, and wine. We participated in a series of meetings with departmental administrators, arranged to have our case presented at meetings we could not attend, and tried to influence other graduate students. Our group grew from an initial five women to involve three-quarters of the women in our department in a variety of ways. During this process of organizing ourselves as female graduate students, we created several documents—memos, cover letters, personal letters.

Such a paper trail is relatively rare. During the following spring, several of us met to write about the events that surrounded and produced these written traces. We spent three hours a week for four months remembering, discussing, rehashing the fall's events, exploring paths not taken, debating "what ifs???" After finding at least preliminary frameworks for understanding what had transpired, we held a series of sessions at which we taped our more or less structured conversations. Two of us then transcribed the tapes and edited them into their present form.

Cathy: I want to begin with something Emma says: History begins with the present; this story we tell of women organizing in a graduate department begins with our current struggle to move from naming the whole—sexism in the academy—to identifying appropriate actions by which to change small pieces of that whole. From where I stand nine months after we began, our narrative does not unravel as a simple tale in which disempowered women students move into empowerment through collective action. We are still asking: Where does it make sense for us to try to effect change and what sort of changes do we want to work for?

Last August, I decided to not return to graduate school. The previous year had been my second year of graduate school and my second institution. Yet I still found myself jettisoning, on a daily basis, the skills and perspectives I had acquired in feminist communities away from academics simply in order to walk into class. The expectation felt clear, although never expressed: Check your feminist consciousness at the door; no room for her here.

When I wrote to the director of graduate studies informing him of my decision to take a leave of absence, I considered covering over my reasons, saying I needed time "to get my head together"; how could he object to that? But I wanted to explain my decision, to communicate the structural problems that confront women in graduate departments. Disempowering and disenabling were the words I used to describe my experience of graduate school in that letter. After he received my letter, our director of graduate studies (DGS) asked to meet with me.

Lots of graduate students take a semester off—nothing unusual about that. For some women in our graduate department, my "individual" decision became a crisis point, the start of "collective" work for structural change. Yet my decision to name what I knew was not enough by itself to provoke a crisis. I did not stand alone. Collective structures already existed among us—groups of women meeting as far back as two years before I came. No one called those structures political, feminist, or even collective: we thought of them as complaining sessions, times to share professional tips, social gatherings. Yet looking back, the crisis point would have been different without them.

Emma: That's certainly true. For as long as I've been a graduate student here, the women in our program met in the student lounge at the beginning of each fall semester. At these get-togethers we met the incoming female students, and touched base among those of us who were returning for another year. These gatherings usually lasted less than an hour, after which we would disperse back to classes and the library. Smaller groups of women committed to feminist ideas and lives met more regularly and frequently to discuss our work and experiences over countless sodas, lunches, and walks to the parking lot. When Cathy made public her decision to leave, we already possessed ways of working with and supporting each other. In a variety of combinations we were friends, classmates, housemates. I guess what typified most of these meetings and relationships was our clarity about our experiences in graduate school and our frustrations, angers, and strategies for dealing with the worst of it. We lacked a sense of possibility that by working together we could really change anything.

I come from a background of activism and action, yet at graduate school I lived a gap between my politics and my everyday reality. While I continue an at least minimally activist and resistant life outside the academy, it seemed nearly impossible to connect this life with my studies and career at Duke. It's a dangerous and at times risky matter to organize as feminist women in a specific graduate program and to demand changes for our immediate lives and surroundings. Some time after the process had begun, I realized that this would affect me directly and that I would be much more on the line than ever before.

Cathy: At the suggestion of the director of Women's Studies, I wrote a memo in preparation for my meeting with the director of graduate studies. I wanted to leave something tangible in his hands to which he could refer after I had gone and after the shock had worn off. The memo outlined three structural problems that face institutions when they confront the sexism endemic to their structures.

Memo

Date: August 25, 1989
To: The Director of Graduate Studies
From: Cathy S.

Problem 1: How can we improve the academic situation of women in this department?

a) Hire faculty conversant with the new scholarship on women, especially faculty who generate it.

b) Actively encourage faculty to take advantage of Women's Studies grants to include the new scholarship about women in existing courses.

c) Move beyond the idea that only women do Women's Studies.

Problem 2: How can we eliminate sexual harassment by faculty and male students?

a) Educate about what sexual harassment is. Make explicit statements about what is appropriate behavior and what is not.

b) The deeper issue: Many men do not know how to deal with women as colleagues.

Problem 3: How can we stimulate awareness of the implications of gender construction in the manifold ways in which faculty and students relate, both inside and outside the classroom, so that the process of reflection becomes part of the structures of the department?

a) Gather information through faculty questionnaire.

b) Begin this discussion as part of orientation.

Cathy: Fearing that I would be dismissed as an oversensitive woman who allowed personal problems to interfere with her work, I asked another student to accompany me to that meeting. She wrote a memo which compiled incidents from various conversations that she had held with other women in the department over the past six months.

In that meeting, the director of graduate studies granted me a semester's leave. He also responded at once to the presentation of our experiences in the memo, suggesting that we distribute that memo among other students to see how they responded.

Memo

Date: August 25, 1989
To: The Director of Graduate Studies
From: Women in the Graduate Program
Re: The Experience of Women in This Program

The list below is not complete, nor does it reflect the sentiments of every woman in the graduate program. But it does reflect conversations with a number of women beginning in spring 1989 from various fields and at different stages.

Our goal is to be heard and to be taken seriously. We want to be respected as scholars and as persons, without degradation simply because we are women. We want to pursue our scholarly interests without being dissuaded from such "lightweight" or "illegitimate" feminist scholarship. We want knowledge to be valued, even when it does not conform to "traditional" definitions of knowledge. We want to pursue our graduate study without sexual harassment and restrictive sexual stereotypes. We do not want to be marginalized, patronized, or tokenized, all of which we have experienced in the program. We do not want to work twice as hard to be considered half as good.

With these goals in mind, we see at least two areas to be addressed: the academic and the interpersonal. Hence, we have divided our suggestions into these two large areas.

Academic

1. Hire faculty with interest/expertise in feminist/women's studies (not just females).

2. Offer more courses that deal with gender issues.
3. Encourage faculty to do research in women's studies.
4. Encourage faculty to mainstream their courses through grants from the Duke Women's Studies Program.
5. Encourage faculty and students to remain current in feminist literature in their fields and not treat such scholarship as a joke or a fad.
6. Encourage (require?) faculty and students to attend seminars/lectures on feminist scholarship.
7. Encourage faculty to include works by and about women on their syllabi and to address gender issues seriously in the classroom.
8. Encourage faculty and students not to dismiss gender studies in religion as partisan, ideological, misguided, marginal, and/or professional suicide, but to take it seriously as a viable area of scholarly endeavor.

Interpersonal

1. Require faculty and students to attend seminars/lectures on what constitutes sexual harassment/sexism, including, but not restricted to: comments about weight, hair, and/or clothing; sexually explicit jokes; heterosexist comments or jokes; close personal scrutiny; exclusive language; patting heads, shoulders, knees; comments that betray sexual stereotypes ("When are you going to get married and have kids?"); tokenizing comments ("Oh, you're a woman, you'll get a job easily"). All of the above have been experienced by women in the program in the last three years.
2. Make students and faculty aware of your support for students who confront faculty and other students regarding sexual harassment/sexism.
3. Encourage faculty to set an example in treating women students seriously and respectfully.
4. Encourage faculty and students to discuss classroom dynamics related to gender issues, assuring students of no reprisals.
5. Raise gender issues in orientation and/or proseminars. Make students aware that such issues exist and encourage discussion.
6. Encourage students to discuss their experiences as graduate students, in order for women and men to understand each other's perspectives, i.e., use of lounge, body language, feelings of being tokenized.
7. Discuss gender issues as they relate to applying for jobs, preparing for interviews, attending professional meetings, negotiating salaries,

being a junior faculty member, and advancing professionally—with both female and male students.

8. Encourage faculty and students not to dismiss sexual harassment/sexism as hysterical, overreacting, inevitable, man-hating, and/or to be tolerated ("Boys will be boys"), but to take it seriously as a violation of human rights. _____

Emma: Cathy met with the director of graduate studies on a Friday, classes started on Monday. To ready the memo for distribution among students and faculty in our program, we composed an introductory cover letter. The process of jointly writing it became the first collective act done by all five of us. Our prior relations and networks shifted to become actively political. . . . I remember the emotion of our work that deadline-strained weekend. We wanted to finish the cover letter and memo and place them in mailboxes on the first day of classes to make clear from the start that feminism and gender were on the year's agenda.

_____

Memo

To: All Graduate Students in the Department
From: Several Women in the Graduate Department
Date: August 28, 1989

This spring and summer several women in the department met to discuss our experiences as women in our program. As we talked and listened to one another, we discovered similar concerns, fears, and disappointments— across fields and at differing stages in the program. Based on these conversations, we wrote the enclosed memo and shared it with [the director of graduate studies] last week. With his support, we decided to circulate the memo among all graduate students in order to face the situation together.

Briefly, we recognize a problem in our department that affects us all. It shapes how we learn and how we are taught, as well as how we perceive, behave, and interact with one another and with the faculty. Because this issue is difficult for all of us to deal with, women and men, many of us have remained silent.

In order to address this problem, all of us must work together. Please read the enclosed memo which outlines some basic facets of the problem, and contact us with your ideas.

We are compiling this information in order to better understand the experiences of students in different fields and to address our concerns concretely. You may remain anonymous if you wish; we will keep your responses confidential. If you indicate your willingness to have your comments shared, we will contact you before disclosing any part of your response. Additionally, if you are interested in specific activities such as seminars, workshops, and/or reading groups, please let us know.

Emma: One of the things we debated and learned through the process of writing these documents was how we communicated our ideas about gender, feminism, and our experiences through language. Now when I read this cover letter, I notice how we used such understated language. We spoke of "problems," general "bad experiences." We told about "concerns, fears, and disappointments." We didn't use the word *feminism*, and we didn't talk about gender, sexism, or our analyses of them. The letter speaks with suggestions of possibility, with hesitation and some tentativeness.

Cathy: When we wrote the cover letter, we made a conscious decision to say nothing that might dissuade a reader from turning the page. We were unsure how to communicate effectively with people who have little awareness of the various analyses and perspectives that feminists have developed to speak about how gender is socially constructed and the ways in which academic institutions perpetuate that system.

Emma: As well as honing the language we used to explain the structural nature of gender bias and sexism, we were figuring out what specific features and aspects of our department needed to be revised in ways beneficial to us. We began this process of organizing with ideals about woman-centered and nonsexist culture and institutions, and with knowledge and anger at the sexist reality of our immediate environment. We soon needed to figure out the specifics, the steps of every size which together might transform the unacceptable.

The letter sent to the departmental executive committee ended with a list of changes and policies they could implement. To create this list we brainstormed things which seemed feasible, at least. As it turned out, the committee later granted us some of these "feasible" suggestions, most of which were absolutely unrelated to any real improvement for our educations and lives as women, or for creating more space for feminist studies.

Memo

Date: September 25, 1989
To: The Executive Committee
Re: The chilly climate for some women in our graduate program

Several weeks ago, a female student decided to take a leave of absence because she found her experience as a woman in the department to be disempowering. As a result, [the director of graduate studies] requested a meeting to discuss sexism in our program. In preparation for that meeting, a number of women, named and unnamed, met and wrote a memo (dated August 28, see enclosure) outlining the problems they perceived. At the suggestion of [the director of graduate studies] we distributed that memo to students and faculty, asking for their comments and suggestions on how to create a more workable environment for both women and men. This second memo represents the next phase: it assesses the responses to our first memo and sets forth the beginnings of an agenda for the future.

No one in our department openly declares that women should remain subordinate to men. However, feminist concerns generally receive only passing notice as an important question for the academic community. Most of the responses we received shared this outlook. While many of our colleagues expressed their support for our agenda, most failed to see the magnitude or the systemic nature of the problem. For example, the experience of a female student whose male professor touches her knee behind closed doors while asking her a personal (and inappropriate) question cannot be equated with the experience of a male student who touches another student's knee in compassion. One man who likened the two episodes clearly does not understand the threat which such touching and remarks present to women—especially in a private situation and from someone with significant authority or power.

Similarly, several colleagues advised us to approach problematic professors and colleagues individually. This solution indicates that they have not yet grasped the scope of the problem. Those who advocate such a course of action remain unaware of the number of such discussions and confrontations both in the classroom and in professors' offices over the past several years. Neither do they seem aware of the undeserved risks and vulnerability such action requires of women—from being labeled a troublemaker to actual reduction of course grades. To suggest that women alone should bear the responsibility of changing the current environment by responding individually to every incident of gender harassment and

146

exclusion of the new scholarship on women in our curriculum implies several things: First, it ignores the systemic nature of the problem. Second, it places the burden to correct the current environment solely on women. Since we all agree that change needs to happen, we should all, male and female, take responsibility for effecting such change. For feminist students and professors to accept the responsibility to "raise consciousness" denies others their responsibility to actively pursue their own education.

We see education as the key to change. To grant a student a doctorate from Duke without any familiarity with feminist methodology, scholarship, and pedagogy handicaps that student by ideologically limiting their education. We cannot expect our professors and colleagues, female and male, to hear and respond immediately to our critiques and visions. Without a common language, we cannot detect something as invisible as the social construction of gender, much less improve the currently unacceptable environment for women in our department. Many of the responses to our first memo stressed education; some mentioned either the required field seminars or a general departmental seminar as possibilities. We underscore these suggestions.

As women in this graduate program we seek inclusion at every level of this department and suggest the following list of actions as first steps to achieving this goal:

1. Fund a work-study position for an ombudsperson. This person would be available for those who feel they have experienced sexual harassment to speak with confidentially. The position includes the responsibility of maintaining records, and, if necessary, finding ways to address particular situations without legal recourse. This person might work with the University Task Force on sexual harassment.
2. Fund a work-study position for a student to address issues of gender construction during orientation week. This person would also distribute the Duke University policies on sexual harassment and inclusive language during orientation.
3. Include discussion of feminist approach and the new scholarship on women in the curriculum, particularly in the required field seminars.
4. Provide access to course syllabi before students sign up for classes. In this way we would know whether the class will include new scholarship on women and could address that issue with the professor prior to the beginning of classes. These syllabi can be collected and kept on file in the department office.
5. Brainstorm about ways in which to make the program more welcoming

to women. Few women apply to this department, and certain fields consistently matriculate embarrassingly small numbers of women. These numbers lead us to believe that people outside of the Duke community also recognize this department as having an untenable climate for women.

6. Mandatory classroom evaluations for all graduate courses. These should be drawn up by students so that they reflect our needs.

7. Inclusion of students in all departmental decision-making bodies, such as the executive committee. This would enable students to take a more active and responsible role in our education.

Cathy: Naming how our experiences as female graduate students differed from those of our male colleagues helped me listen to my own voice. These experiences had remained unspoken for a long time, even among ourselves. Yet when I look back, I see that we had little choice about placing our experiences in the forefront of our arguments. I remember how differently the director of graduate studies received the first two memos: the memo which focused upon our experiences evoked immediate enthusiasm whereas the memo which focused upon structural problems got little reaction.

People in our department would acknowledge that we'd had bad experiences—especially if they thought these experiences concerned sexual harassment. The university has developed a policy for dealing with sexual harassment; administrators have handled that particular problem before. By contrast, *gender harassment* constituted a term with which they were not familiar and for which they had no official guideline.

We had initiated dialogue about the differences between men's and women's experiences as graduate students. Yet discussion rarely moved to the systemic level. Basing our arguments on our different experiences as women allowed specific examples and the question of numbers (How many women "feel" this way?) to remain the primary issue. As a result of this focus upon individuals, we were asked to name the names of problematic professors, rather than engage in a discussion about the various ways in which gender socialization denies both professors and students access to appropriate models for treating women as colleagues/students. Similarly, our memos and reports were often placed alongside the experiences of nonfeminist women who gave glowing accounts of the same program we were criticizing in order to block or invalidate our claims.

When rehashing the fall's events, we debated whether our arguments might not have gotten a little further if we had placed the claim that sexism is a broader sociocultural institution in the forefront—and only within that framework, recounted our experiences as symptoms of how the larger sex-gender system functions in graduate departments.

The operative words here are, of course, "a little further." No arguments, however clearly we state them, will persuade an institution to admit a "mistake" and commit wholeheartedly to eradicating structural sexism. Such change requires collective action.

Emma: Our strategies for actions kept changing as we found different sites on which to focus. These sites of actions varied in the degree to which they were open, general, public, more intimate, private, self-focused, administratively focused, peer-focused. Almost all our attention remained on the members of a fairly large graduate department, yet within this domain there were choices to be made: What combination of private discussions with people holding power, group meetings with allies, one-on-one hallway discussions with our peers, and so on, should we pursue? Our first memo, distributed department-wide, raised lots of discussion and debate, and generated written responses to us and to administrators. From there, it seems that we pursued increasingly private and quieter actions. We met with individual faculty in specific fields, wrote memos addressed to specific and small groups, and prepared for meetings which took place behind increasingly closed doors.

Nearly everything we did up to and including presenting our claims to the executive committee and later meetings with several administrators was done at someone else's suggestion. After this meeting, we began to select our sites and actions more carefully and to figure out more specifically where to put our attention and energies.

In November, three of us decided to do a project in public view. Skimming through the schedule of the upcoming national conference for our field, we photocopied every page which included feminist topics. Believe me, we were surprised at how many we found. With brightly colored magic markers we highlighted all of the feminist presentations, papers, roundtables, films, and papered all four walls of our department's student lounge with them. This was a particularly appropriate location for an action because several years back female students had organized around their informal exclusion from this space. After papering the four walls we put a sign on the door which asked: "Don't know where to start?" Then, as one entered the lounge on the facing wall, over a large portrait of a white, male, Christian professor emeritus we placed in a speaking bubble the words "This guy says: Check out the feminist scholarship at this year's convention!"

This action represented to us a chance to move our focus away from administrative sites, to make our issues and claims more visible, and to try to transform the culture of the program. Since the lounge is filled with patriarchal portraits it was thrilling to appropriate one as our ally.

Cathy: By the end of the fall semester, eleven out of the fifteen women in the department had involved themselves in some way. Extending the annual beginning of the year get-together, we held several meetings in our homes to which many women came. While I wanted this group to share women-centered space and process (many women in the department had never done that), this also meant struggling with how to relate to women who didn't identify as I do. We differ from one another in many ways: religious and cultural backgrounds, present commitments, family involvements, class backgrounds, sexual preferences, academic methods, and feminist commitments.

By spring some wanted to shift the focus from memo writing and meetings to figuring out specific sites in the department where we wanted to work for change. The shift brought out dissension, only some of which can I name. First, there were conflicting desires about what the group should do. A shift threatened to leave other women out—women who primarily wanted support; women who couldn't act politically for numerous reasons such as family commitments; women who thought such action too risky. On my part I wanted to share intellectual work; strategize steps for change; and find support as I sought to create space in my classes for my own feminist work.

Second, the shift meant confronting the many ways in which we dismiss our insights as "complaining" rather than strategize together to create conditions so that we do not have to feel this way.

Third, confronting differences among ourselves also meant acknowledging and accepting the existence of lines we will not cross, risks we will not take. Each of us has identified in different ways with the structures we seek to change. From my standpoint now, I see the process of gaining identity through academic disciplines as one of limiting our ability to use the various voices we were developing.

Emma: Right at the end of the semester, as most of us were scrambling to finish papers, classes, grading, a memo appeared in our mailboxes from the executive committee of our department.

The memo recalled briefly the series of meetings that semester at which gender had been discussed. It emphasized the good will and openness on everyone's part to talk about the issues we had raised.

The authors of the memo said that we had "expressed concern" about several things: the absence, repudiation, and disparagement of feminist scholarship in our classrooms; the overall attractiveness, or unattractiveness, of this program for women; and the need for the number of women in the program to increase. Their memo repeated our distinction between sexual harassment and gender harassment, putting "gender harassment" in quotation marks as if they were not yet comfortable with this phrase to which we had introduced them.

Following this, the committee members summarized their discussions and suggestions: they were concerned about "inappropriate behavior," and they considered feminist scholarship to raise issues of importance for all graduate students. They promised to keep files of syllabi for graduate courses, to distribute course evaluations in order to gain more information, and to explore ways to increase the numbers of feminist graduate students.

Well. After everything we had done, it was hard to react in any way but cynically to this memo. Only with time have I been able to agree partially with those who considered the memo to be quite a "victory." I suppose it is. A victory to know that our words and arguments and voices had been heard, debated, recapitulated, and rewritten into a memo sent from "the other side." While I appreciate their response, I have doubts about how well our issues had been communicated. Their recapitulation of our voices was their recapitulation: their priorities differed from ours, as did their understanding of the depth and ramifications.

Our attempts to raise gender issues and create change could have had many results. In responding to the claims that we made, the committee had many choices. It opted to respond in print. The danger of a memo is that it can easily stay a memo; as far as I know, several of the committee's resolutions were not put into effect.

As a result of our work and actions around the department, things did change. While little of this change resulted from the contents of the administrators' memo, I think that the presence of the memo became part of a tendency around our department that recognized some of our feminist claims.

Cathy and Emma: Friends ask us if our work that fall was worthwhile, and inquire whether anything has changed. The question and our answer are simultaneously simple and ambiguous. Were the time and energy and risks worthwhile? It was worthwhile to help start a feminist struggle. For it is a struggle, and naming it so we recall how we used to see this process as ongoing cycles of taking an action, recoiling, changing, taking more action. Our open collective of feminist women continues, not a one-time phenomenon ending with a semester. We didn't stop in December. The lessons learned about language, communication, effective arguments, finding allies, and figuring strategy continue to serve us well as we integrate feminist political commitments into our academic lives and identities. Groups still meet very regularly to talk about our work and our lives, trade information, strategize and organize our active responses to current events in the department. And, as hard as it is to quantify, we did put feminist issues at the center of attention at several department-wide meetings and leave them on people's minds. We made gender into a contested issue, and sustained the contest for several months.

Have things changed? We sometimes find more acceptance and latitude to do feminist work. We've created stronger feminist networks to sustain us now and in the future. But as Cathy said before, our narrative is not one in which feminist collective action results in empowerment and systemic change. We still find ourselves battling over inclusion, over harassment, over the legitimacy and centrality of women's experiences and feminist scholarship, knowing that these things will only begin to change as many feminist and not-yet feminist women and their allies organize and work collectively everywhere.

THE EVOLUTION AND PROCESS OF A SUCCESSFUL GRADUATE FEMINIST READING GROUP

*Suzanne Franks Shedd, Shelley Park, Elana Newman,
Michelle A. LaRocque, Angela Hubler, Melissa Haussman,
Anne S. Forrest, and Gillian Brock*

In the fall of 1987, the Women's Studies Program circulated a memo among graduate students interested in feminist scholarship. The memo mentioned, among other things, current openings in established feminist reading groups and the formation of new feminist reading groups.

Few of us can explain precisely what motivated us to respond to the memo. Perhaps we all had some need for a feminist space, although it is doubtful that any of us would have expressed our need in that way at the time. The program had been working at establishing reading groups as an extracurricular supplement to Women's Studies curricular activities for several years—probably more aware of this need of female graduate students than we, ourselves, were. But despite our relative inarticulateness concerning our motivations for forming a reading group, nine of us began meeting biweekly in the Ninth Street Bakery to discuss randomly selected feminist articles. Of the original nine students, six remain. The three who left all left within the first term, and two members joined us shortly thereafter.

Our current members represent a variety of disciplinary backgrounds and interests—four members are in disciplines in the humanities, three members are social scientists, and one member is a "hard" scientist. We are also at different stages in our academic programs, with some members close to finishing and others just past prelims. Furthermore, our involvement with the Women's Studies Program varies. Some of us have or are pursuing a Women's Studies certificate, others have designed, taught, or graded Women's Studies classes, and others have been only peripherally involved with the program.

In addition, we come from different regional and/or national backgrounds, as well as different class backgrounds. We represent a range of lower-middle to upper-class family histories and a range of present financial struggles, as we attempt to work our way—as graders, teachers, scholarship recipients, workers in private enterprise or private practice—through graduate school. Our present personal narratives also differ: some members are married, others are involved in long-term heterosexual or lesbian relationships, and yet others are contentedly unattached.

Finally, we occupy a variety of positions, from moderate to radical, in our approaches to, and applications of, feminist theory. Our political involvements range from participation in classroom, departmental, and wider campus politics to activity in local, national, and international political struggles. And our concerns range from issues of academic and workplace freedom to issues of sexual and reproductive freedom to the overthrow of the patriarchal, capitalistic state. Despite all of these differences, we have over the past two years become a cohesive group.

What follows is a brief narrative and analysis of our evolution as a group. Although we describe this evolution in terms of "stages" and "phases," we would like to note that we are dividing a gradual, continuous process of development into useful intellectual constructs. Thus, we are not describing discrete stages of development per se. Furthermore, the evolution of the group does not coincide in any neat way with the development of individual members. We have tried to focus upon those aspects of our experience that could be generalized so that it might be of help to other feminist graduate students who are interested in developing interdisciplinary reading groups. One of the aims of feminism has been to break down disciplinary boundaries and to overcome the "territorial" approach to knowledge that is prevalent in the academy. We will begin by describing our efforts to realize this aspect of the feminist transformation of knowledge.

One of Matt Groenig's "School is Hell" cartoons captures the first difficulty in establishing any sort of interdisciplinary reading group. There he offers this true/false question as a test of one's fitness for graduate school: "My idea of a good time is using jargon and citing authorities." Being committed, at least in theory, to communicating with one another, we were nevertheless faced with some formidable communication obstacles. The first step was relatively easy: avoiding the conscious use of jargon which is designed to exclude outsiders as much as to communicate with insiders. There were inevitably times, however, when one woman's crystalline thought was another woman's mud. For example, our literary critic's brilliant discourse on "texts" went right by our psychologist, who, not being exposed to cutting-edge literary theory, had an old-fashioned view of a "text" as something like a "written document."

The resulting calls for help generally led to clearer explanations through a process of translation. We searched for metaphors and descriptions that could be understood by each of us. This was the stage where each of us took turns describing our particular view of the elephant. At times this could be uncomfortable—it often seemed as though we were describing alien existences to each other. But as we each learned more of the others' viewpoints, translation shifted from a "*chapeau*-means-hat" mode to one where we described different kinds of hats and how they came to be worn, and how what might look like a hat to one member was actually a scarf to another, and so on.

In the earlier stages of the group, if our reading came from a clearly defined discipline, we would call upon the appropriate member to play the role of expert, and then we would each add our own view to her analysis. If the reading was not so clearly defined, we would each offer the appropriate analysis from our still isolated perspectives. In either case, we would try to "step outside of ourselves" and adopt someone else's disciplinary perspective. We would, for a moment, try to think like a literary critic (or a philosopher, or an economist). Such attempts usually lasted only a moment, with each of us quickly returning to our known and comfortable position.

Since connections between members were relatively undeveloped, there was some fear of commenting on things seen as outside of one's area of expertise. This, in turn, led to a general preference for drawing the "expert opinion" out of the appropriate person. At this time, then, our individual identities were primarily in terms of our disciplinary identities, and the group voice was more like a series of solos, some longer than others.

Yet, we eventually began to see how, for example, psychological principles could offer explanation and understanding of ideas and practices in science, or how literary criticism might be of use in philosophy. The group voice evolved as we learned not just to offer our perspectives to others' projects, but to examine our own projects with newly developed perspectives. Both methods of working together are important and useful, but the latter method is the gift we have created for ourselves as a group. We have progressed from offering our expertise on a topic to understanding someone else's ideas on that topic to collecting viewpoints and fashioning a new image of things previously seen through a single lens.

This development of a common language enabled us to create a feminist space where we felt secure. Being able to communicate across disciplinary lines gave back to each of us parts of ourselves that had been repressed by the process of professionalization within our own disciplines. Being able to think and speak outside of our rigid academic boundaries allowed us to start interacting with each other as *persons* rather than as professionals. For example, we began inviting each other into our homes for potluck dinners, and we began to take a deeper interest in each others' lives.

This process could be described as the beginning of friendship—a form of human interaction that is often lacking in the academic environment. It is difficult, as graduate students, to find people who are interested in knowing us as individuals—our professors generally have little interest in anything but our thoughts on *their* work, and our students cannot help seeing us as authority figures of some form or other (the mother figure, for most of us). And, if a department encourages competition amongst its graduate students, then there will be severe limits on the possibilities for developing friendships with fellow graduate students. Furthermore, the fact of being a woman in a male-dominated discipline creates needs that are not, and will not be, shared by our male peers. And finally, since we work in environments that are often hostile to feminism, we find ourselves in alienated and defensive positions.

At this point in our evolution as a group, we downplayed both potential and actual sources of conflict between members of the group. Since we were all committed to establishing for ourselves a feminist space where we felt legitimated as feminists and "safe" from the "outside" world, we were willing to overlook potentially destructive undercurrents in our group dynamics. One article in particular has helped us come to understand what we were doing at this point in our group history. Bernice Johnson Reagon writes: "Now every once in awhile there is a need for people to clean our corners and bar the doors and check everybody who comes in the door, and check what they carry in and say, 'Humph, inside this place the only thing we are going to deal with is X or Y or Z.' And so only the Xs or Ys or Zs get to come in. That place can become a nurturing place or a very destructive place. Most of the time when people do that, they do it because of the heat of trying to live in this society where being an X or Y or Z is very difficult, to say the least." She calls this process that of building a "home" for oneself, and that is what we were doing. We made a place for ourselves that was a nurturing place, where we could try to compensate for the indifference and hostility that we encountered on a daily basis in our academic lives. However, Reagon also notes that such space can become a destructive place, and we are now coming to a point where we can begin to explore the "underside" of our "happy home."

Now that we have established this safe, protective space that we can claim as our own arena for feminist discourse, the function of the group has started to change. These changes were not planned, acknowledged, or named until we collaborated on this paper. Conflict became evident when the possibility of introducing a new member into the group was discussed. At that point, we began to reflect upon the role of the reading group in our lives. While some members saw the introduction of someone new as an extending of the home, others saw it as threatening. We began to explore these different conceptions of our reading group, and we began to work toward a vision that would be comfortable but nonexclusionary.

We now envision our current phase as "coalition-building," another phrase we have borrowed from Bernice Reagon. Coalition-building requires the recognition of conflict and of the differences between individual members. In addition, it binds people together as *allies*, and not merely as friends.

This coalition-building is difficult work; as we try to challenge ourselves, we discover that our group is becoming increasingly more unsafe because we are taking risks with ourselves, each other, and our values. The realization that differences would not destroy our shared commitment to feminism has enabled us to take a more critical stance toward individual pieces of scholarship. It has also enabled us to explore the connections between feminist theory and feminist practice in ways that we had not previously considered. Our increased ability to offer and receive criticism has aided us in the presentation of our own work within the group. We are empowered by this progression and feel energized to continue our lives as academic women.

In creating a home for ourselves, we were also constructing a model of what academic discourse should be. In many ways, the assumptions, process, and structure of our reading group directly oppose the dominant values of the academy and even of society in general. However, we are beginning to discover the ways in which we have internalized some of the assumptions we wish to reject. Based on these assumptions, we have reproduced some dominant societal "norms" within the group.

We realize that we have assumed, but not acknowledged, certain "norms" for participation within the group. For example, vocal members of the group identified less vocal members as having a "problem" with participation and as not "contributing" as much to the group. In some ways we reproduced the "male" model of participation, defining participation as "shouting the longest and the loudest." We thus reinforced one of the dominant assumptions at work in academic discourse: that being a good listener somehow means that one is neither "participating" in nor "contributing" to the discussion.

Since many of us feel silenced in the normal space in which we live our intellectual, political, and personal lives, the ability to speak in a feminist space is liberating; however, we may have to learn *how* to speak in such a space, taking care not to carry over the value scheme in operation in our academic environments. This means recognizing that learning and listening are not mutually exclusive activities, and it also means understanding that "making noise" and "having something to say" are not synonymous.

This competitive model of "discussion" is problematic in another way: those individuals who shout the loudest may not be shouting about issues that the group as a whole is concerned with. So, not only do some people end up dominating the discussion, they also end up determining *what* is to be discussed. The values of the "dominant" members of the group became the norm not only in terms of evaluation of participation levels, but also in terms of sexual and relational preference. The most vocal members of the group, who are heterosexual and married, defined issues of relationships in exclusionary ways.

We reproduced the oppressive behavior of mainstream society in part because we reproduced yet another oppressive hierarchy, that of the public over the private. In our choice of readings, we established academic concerns as central and personal issues as peripheral, in part because we are all academics, and many of us came to know each other in an academic rather than in a social setting. This priority was also evidenced in the temporal structure of our meetings—we would chitchat for a while, then do some "serious" work, and then return to chitchat before parting. Had we brought the "peripheral" concerns of our relationships and personal lives into the center of discussion, we might have taken responsibility for our heterosexism and marriagism. Furthermore, we might have alleviated some of the guilt associated with the discussion of "trivial" matters.

The discussion of these issues in our group grew out of a labeling of some group members as "strong" and other group members as "weak," coupled with an unacknowledged equating of "strong" with "good" and "weak" with "bad." The strong/weak dichotomy was swiftly replaced with the vocal/nonvocal dichotomy as we began to talk about this previously unrecognized "problem." When we had hashed out the vocality issues, however, we came back to our original strong/weak terminology and found it had acquired a new meaning.

We are *all* strong women; we must be, to have survived so far in the academy. The reading group provided a place we could go for support, encouragement, and refreshment. But because the need for support or help was viewed by some of us as "weak" and therefore "bad," we felt reluctant to ask for it. The resulting projection, by some, of a "strong, I don't need help" persona prevented others from feeling that they could or should offer any support. We are striving now for a recognition of our varied qualities of strength, and an acceptance of our needs to give *and* receive help and support.

Our present conception of our group as in a transition from home to coalition means that we cannot make a tidy summary of where we will go from here. We are still working on the issues discussed in this paper, and on articulating our goals as a group and as group members. Where we once saw the reading of feminist works as an end in itself, we now see this as the means to an end less clearly defined. Along the way, praxis has taken on greater importance for us. We want to make a difference in people's lives, beginning with our own.

CONTRIBUTORS

Note: Though some of the contributions to *Engaging Feminism* appear with pseudonyms (first name and initial), all of the contributors agreed to be listed here.

MARY-MALLETTE ACKER: I hope to complete my Master of Arts in liberal studies in the summer of 1991. I anticipate writing my thesis from a feminist perspective on a subject still to be chosen.

MARA ILYSE AMSTER: I'm presently living in Boston, trying to find a job in the field of publishing and debating whether or not to apply to graduate school for a Ph.D. in English literature. To help supplement my long-term goals and aspirations, I'm waitressing and learning the art of mixing oreos into ice cream (amazing what a Duke education prepares one for!).

EILEEN ALEXA ANDERSON: I'm currently preparing for graduate school in clinical psychology with a feminist and cross-cultural emphasis on women and their issues, transitions, and empowerment.

MARY ARMSTRONG: I am particularly interested in sexuality and gender issues in the Victorian novel, especially the development of lesbian theory/writing. I hope to be teaching English literature and women's studies in the near future.

MICHELLE BEATY: I am a political science major in the process of applying to law schools. I plan to practice in public interest law although I'm not sure in exactly what capacity. My ultimate goal is to become a judge. I know that I would not be happy in a career that did not connect me directly with people. I enjoy reading just about anything and I cannot live without music (especially jazz).

MARY R. BOWMAN: I am currently completing a Ph.D. in English at Duke University. My principal academic interests are sixteenth-century literature and women's studies.

GINGER BRENT: All of my work relates in some way to the issue of literacy. Ultimately, I hope to teach at the secondary school level, so currently I am writing a dissertation on young adult fiction as a way to familiarize myself with the material that's been written to appeal to thirteen to eighteen year olds. This year I plan to defend that dissertation, to earn my secondary school teacher's certificate, and to teach at Eastern Michigan University.

LYNN E. BROADDUS: I researched male sterility (in plants) after a first career teaching science in a girl's boarding school. I now intend to pursue a career in science and education policy.

GILLIAN BROCK: I am interested in ethical naturalism and moral epistemology and their implications for feminist theory.

ANN BURLEIN: I am a student in the Religion and Culture Program at Duke University. I'm currently writing a paper which analyzes the conflictual processes that stand behind "identity" and their elaboration into diverse tactics of disidentification (from privilege, from persona created as a necessary condition for performing a professional role, from victim identification and its politics of despair).

DEBORAH K. CHAPPEL: I am a Ph.D. candidate in English at Duke University. I am writing my dissertation on the history of popular American women's romance and its intersections with American feminism.

KERITH COHEN: I am a history major and am working toward my women's studies certificate. I plan to attend law school and use my degree to fight sexual discrimination.

APRIL CONNER: My academic interests include sociology and political science, my double major during my undergraduate years at Duke. I plan to go on to law school in the pursuit of a career in corporate law.

CYNTHIA J. DAVIS: I am currently in my third and final year of graduate course work in the Department of English at Duke. My primary interests are feminist theory and the novel, with a particular emphasis on American women writers. For my dissertation, I would like to explore specific narratives of gender and the body in American novels and the significance and consequences of their differences from each other.

MARTINE DEVOS: I work primarily on late nineteenth- and early twentieth-century American literature, with special emphasis on theories and representations of gender and class.

JUDITH W. DORMINEY: I am presently earning a Master of Social Work degree at the University of North Carolina at Chapel Hill. I am specializing in aging with an emphasis on older women's issues.

KIM DOWELL: My career aspirations are to become a child psychologist. I would like to work with kids of all backgrounds, but I want to focus most of my energies on black and disadvantaged and abused children.

REBECCA DUNN: Currently, I'm working on my dissertation research in the field of molecular genetics studying gene regulation in *Drosophila*. That is, I spend lots of time raising, counting, grinding, sorting, and mating millions of fruit flies.

LUCY EDWARDS: At the time this journal entry was written, I was a third-year graduate student in early Christian history, with aspirations for a Ph.D. and a pleasant job teaching bright young students at a well-endowed college or university. This position would materially support my desire to take the study of religion into public high schools, with the hope of helping adolescents make a happy marriage between critical thinking and whatever spiritual faith they choose to accept (or reject).

MECHELLE R. EVANS: I graduated from Duke in May 1990, receiving a B.A. in history. I am presently a first-year law student at the New York University School of Law. I plan to concentrate in international law. One day, I plan to use my law degree and legal training in politics to help further the goals of women and other minorities throughout the world.

KATHRYN FIRMIN: I am a graduate student in political science studying the political economy of development in Africa. In my own research, I advance a deliberately interdisciplinary perspective, integrating elements of political science, economics, anthropology, history, and women's studies in an effort to address political issues more completely.

ANNE S. FORREST: I am interested in the relationships between government and industry. My research examines the success of in-

formation programs as an alternative to traditional regulation of
environmental pollution.

ERIN L. GIBSON: I am a junior majoring in public policy studies/psychol-
ogy. I have a great interest in social problems, and I am considering
a career in social policy or health policy.

JONATHAN GROTENSTEIN: I'm a double major in philosophy and economics in my junior year. After graduation, I hope to do some
traveling and some working. My long-range goal is to avoid becoming a burden on my parents.

MELISSA HAUSSMAN: A central research problem for me is that U.S.
women's status in public life is lower than in many other indus-
trialized Western democracies. This is measured by the dearth of
elected women officials and by the lack of a constitutional equality
guarantee. My goals are to finish my dissertation, emerge from
graduate school relatively sane, and find a teaching job where I
can combine my women-in-politics and women's studies interests.

BARBARA G. HEGGIE: I am a lawyer. I wish to use my skills and license to
achieve measures of justice, particularly for women.

HEATHER H. HOWARD: Presently I am working in Washington, D.C., for
Congresswoman Nita M. Lowey. Ultimately I would love to work on
the Hill doing legislative work in the issues of foreign policy and
women's issues. I plan to attend the Johns Hopkins School of International Studies in pursuit of a Master's in international relations
next year. Alternately though, I am becoming interested in issues
in international education (I teach ESL on the side) and could be
convinced to go abroad to teach.

ANGELA HUBLER: I am A.B.D. (all but dissertation) in English at Duke
University. I am currently writing on modernist American women
writers and teaching at Kansas State University.

PATRICK INMAN: My interest centers on the history of primary relationships. I am completing an oral history of the "prolife" movement in
a town in the southern United States. In my Ph.D. thesis I intend to
tell part of the story of a Spanish community and its "guest worker"
transplants in Germany between 1939 and the late 1970s. I am
a graduate student in European history at the University of North
Carolina at Chapel Hill.

KATIE KENT: I am a graduate student in English. My research interests include feminist and gay/lesbian theory and the writing of modernist
women, especially Gertrude Stein.

CONTRIBUTORS

CATHERINE B. KLEINER: I am currently an instructor in the history department at Deerfield Academy in Deerfield, Massachusetts. I teach two survey courses—one in U.S. history and another in Western civilizations—to high school students. Just two years ago, Deerfield was an all male institution. Needless to say, I have encountered some resistance from male students who say I am "biased" any time I mention women. Eventually I hope to reenter a graduate program in history and earn a Ph.D. I would then like to do either museum work or college-level teaching.

MICHELLE A. LAROCQUE: I am currently working on a dissertation in philosophy. My area of specialization is personal identity and theories of the self. My future projects will focus on the history of women in philosophy.

LIZ MORGAN: Having graduated from Duke with a history degree and a certificate in women's studies, I hope to pursue a career in writing and editing.

ALICE NELSON: My principal academic/teaching interest is the intersection of Spanish American literature and Spanish American feminist thought. My dissertation deals with the cultural impact of the Chilean women's movement on literary texts produced during the Pinochet dictatorship.

DIANA LEIGH NELSON: I graduated cum laude in May of 1990 with degrees in political science and history and a concentration in the arts. My future plans include a law degree and a career in the entertainment industry, I hope, writing and producing films.

MARIE E. NELSON: I am presently developing a political science degree with a concentration in international security and the Third World. I am a junior at Duke University, and have also studied at the London School of Economics and Political Science and at Howard University. I plan to attend law school upon graduation and hope to pursue a career in international civil rights law.

ELANA NEWMAN: I am a clinical psychology doctoral student who specializes in understanding the effects of recovery process from sexual trauma. In addition, I study the history of women in psychology and general issues in the psychology of women.

CLAIRE O'BARR: I graduated from Duke in 1990 with a Bachelor's degree in art history and a concentration in women's studies. I am currently working for the Women's Law and Public Policy Fellowship Program in Washington, D.C.

CHARLES PAINE: I am currently researching the role of the humanities in nineteenth- and twentieth-century American education, especially the politics of composition philosophy and literacy.

SHELLEY PARK: I am primarily interested in the ethical and political presuppositions of theories of human nature, the mind, and personhood and in what those assumptions reflect about the social and biological embodiment of traditional and contemporary philosophers.

CONNIE E. PEARCY: I plan to graduate in December of 1990 with a history degree and a certificate in women's studies. I am interested in learning more about the public education system, electoral politics, political activism, and life before I begin working on a Ph.D. in history.

MIRIAM PESKOWITZ: I am a graduate student in the Department of Religion, writing a dissertation which explores the intersections between religious ideologies of work and sexuality and the everyday lives of Jewish female workers. Combining "study" with "action," I work at Durham's Rape Crisis Center, organize against militarism and military actions, and write articles for Duke's alternative news media.

CYNTHIA L. RANDALL: I am a first-year law student at the University of Pennsylvania. I have an M.A. in English and an ongoing interest in literature, politics, and feminism.

KATHY RUDY: I am a graduate student in Christian ethics, interested primarily in sexual ethics and issues of marriage and family. The feminist movement gave me the strength to make it through seminary and continues to help me find my rightful place in the Christian church.

MICHAEL W. RUIZ: I would like to continue my education by working toward a Master's in architecture after earning a B.A. in history and art history at Duke.

ELIZABETH S. SAYRE: I am interested in language teaching, nineteenth- and twentieth-century French literature, and women's autobiography.

ANNE CHANDLER SCOTT: I am currently investigating connections between issues of schooling and eighteenth-century women's fiction. I am also interested in convergences between composition theory and feminist pedagogy.

COLLEEN M. SEGUIN: I am a third-year graduate student in history. My primary academic interest is Tudor-Stuart women's history, particularly the history of women's religious activities. I hope to eventually teach British history and women's studies on the college level.

V. V. SERRANT: I am a sociology/English major. At the present time I am undecided as to which area of graduate work I will concentrate on. As far as career goals are concerned, I am still looking at all of my options.

MIRIAM SHADIS: I am working on my dissertation, which is about Berenguela of Leon and Blanche of Castile, who were thirteenth-century regents, patrons, and sisters. Someday I would like to teach in the fields of European and women's history.

KARLA G. SHARGENT: Working toward a Ph.D. in religion (with a concentration in Hebrew Bible), I hope to teach and work in a small, liberal arts college, especially if it enables me to facilitate work among the departments of religion, history, and women's studies.

SUZANNE FRANKS SHEDD: I work with magnetic resonance spectroscopy in applications to biological systems, and am exploring the connections between feminism and science. My goal is an academic appointment which allows me to continue pursuing both interests.

REID SMITH: I am a graduate student in cultural anthropology at Duke. My interests include formulations of ethnic, religious, and national identities in Muslim East Africa and mass media cultural representations.

BANU SUBRAMANIAM: I work on the maintenance of the flower color polymorphism in the common morning glory (*Ipomoea purpurea*). I am currently also writing an article on objectivity and the sociology of science, influenced by my interest in the feminist critique of science.

SILVIA R. TANDECIARZ: My current research interests include contemporary women writers from the southern cone of Latin America (Argentina, Chile, and Uruguay), and particularly their responses to the repressive military regimes that have governed much of their recent history. I am interested in the intersection between authoritarian politics and narrative voice, and particularly in how the experience of state terror affects the construction and deconstruction of representations of gender in literature. I am especially drawn to the work of Uruguayan Cristina Peri Rossi and of Argentine Luise Valenzuela.

DONNA M. THOMPSON: As one who studies seventeenth- and eighteenth-

century British literature, expounding upon the future places me
in quite a quandary. I hope to continue exploring the past as a college professor. However, for me, anything in this century is still
negotiable.

KAT TURNER: I would like to go into sexual health education and counseling because they form a good meeting point between community
work, psychology, and promoting women's issues.

WENDY WAGNER: I am a graduate student in the Department of English at
Duke University, working on my dissertation in African-American
and American literature.

CARY WATSON: I am a sophomore psychology major and am also interested
in foreign languages and music. I plan to go to graduate school and
pursue a career in psychology.

KATHRYN WEST: My academic interests include the study of the novel,
nineteenth-century British and nineteenth- and twentieth-century
American literature, and women's fiction and history.